LOVE
SIGNALS

LOVE
SIGNALS

A Practical Field Guide to
the Body Language of Courtship

DAVID GIVENS, Ph.D.

ST. MARTIN'S PRESS ☙ NEW YORK

www.stmartins.com

Illustrations by Aaron Huffman

Library of Congress Cataloging-in-Publication Data

Givens, David B.
    Love signals : a practical field guide to the body language of courtship /
David Givens.—1st U.S. ed.
        p. cm.
    Includes bibliographical references (p. 221).
    ISBN 0-312-31505-8
    EAN 978-0312-51505-4
    1. Courtship. 2. Interpersonal attraction. 3. Nonverbal communication.
4. Body language. 5. Mate selection. I. Title.

HQ801.G47 2005
646.7'7—dc22

                                                    2004051200

First Edition: February 2005

10   9   8   7   6   5   4   3   2   1

For Doreen, with love

See, how she leans her cheek upon her hand!
O, that I were a glove upon that hand,
That I might touch that cheek!
—WILLIAM SHAKESPEARE, *ROMEO AND JULIET*

CONTENTS

ACKNOWLEDGMENTS

I would like to thank my colleagues in anthropology, archaeology, biology, linguistics, neuroscience, psychology, semiotics, and sociology, whose research has contributed to the scientific study of courtship presented in *Love Signals*. I would like to thank my literary agent, Eileen Cope of Lowenstein-Yost Associates in New York, for her help and encouragement on this project. Special thanks go to my editor at St. Martin's Press, Diane Reverand, for her enthusiasm and guidance, and to her editorial assistant, Regina Scarpa, for her persistence and patience.

PREFACE

MARIANNE: Oh, come on, Professor. These are just normal
American kids.
PROFESSOR: American, yes. Normal, no. Marianne, they're a
true subculture.

—*BEACH PARTY* (1963)

In the 1963 musical *Beach Party*, actor Robert Cummings plays a
bearded anthropologist who studies the dating rituals of Southern
California's surfing enthusiasts, which he likens to the mating rites of
the North American whooping crane. When not spying through a tel-
escope, he uses a method called *participant observation* to court the leading lady, played by Annette Funicello, in an experiment to see how the
leading man, Frankie Avalon, will react.

Beach Party opens with Dolores (Funicello) and Frankie driving to
the beach for what he thinks will be a romantic vacation for two. Fear-
ful of what might happen, Dolores secretly invites their surfer friends
along to keep them company. Angered by her deception, Frankie flirts
with another woman to make Dolores jealous. When Dolores retali-
ates by flirting with Professor Robert Sutwell (Cummings), Frankie's
plan backfires.

Beach Party was first in a series of movies set on California beaches
to depict the clothing, hairstyles, language, music, and wild, gyrating
dances of the indigenous surfing scene. The movie was very unscien-
tific and all in fun.

As a freshman majoring in anthropology at San Diego State College, I couldn't have known that I would one day become an anthropologist who would study the body language of courtship. Nor would I have believed that so much of what I had seen in *Beach Party* was true. The professor's comparison of surfers to whooping cranes, for instance, has a factual basis in biology. Much of our courtship is rooted in the evolution of vertebrates. To lure a mate, we use many of the same body movements, gestures, and postures used by reptiles, mammals, and birds.

A case in point is dance. Whooping cranes court by flapping their wings, bowing their heads, and leaping into the air. The male struts in a high-stepping gait, stomps his feet, tosses his head, and ruffles his feathers to say "Look at me!" An interested female imitates his body movements, dances a duet beside him, bows as he bows, and tosses a twig into the air with her bill. On the beach, nocturnal surfers dance, pump their elbows and arms in unison, rachet their shoulders in tandem, shake their heads, and stamp their feet. They make rhythmic, bowing motions from the waist toward each other to invite physical closeness.

Through a nonverbal lens, the courtship of birds and human beings looks much the same. Both send and receive body-language cues that enable them to move closer together in space. In humans, we call these nonverbal gestures, postures, facial expressions, and clothing cues "love signals."

Love Signals

Love Signals begins with a look at the five phases of courtship. In Phase One, Attracting Attention, you advertise your physical presence, your gender, and your willingness to be approached. In Phase Two, the Recognition Phase, you read how others respond to your bids for attention. Positive feedback invites you ahead to Phase Three, Speech. As you speak, nonverbal messages go back and forth inviting you closer—if all goes well—to Phase Four. In the fourth or Touch Phase, you transcend the logic of words and communicate in a more ancient and more romantic, tactile mode. Finally, if courtship is successful, you validate your sexual bond in Phase Five, Lovemaking. *Love Signals* details the nonverbal signs, signals, and cues you send and receive in each of courtship's five phases.

Next, I examine the essential role your face plays in courtship. You will learn how your features may be optimally displayed. I then decode the language of your body to find silent messages given off by your shoulders, neck, arms, hands, waist, calves, ankles, feet, and toes. Since your body is usually clothed, we will analyze expressive shapes, colors, and markings encoded in arm wear, shoulder wear, leg wear, and shoes. We decipher background messages of spaces, places, and interiors—the physical settings in which you meet—to learn how environs help or hinder the meeting process. Chemical cues emanating from aromas, tastes, steroids, sterols, and hormones strongly shape your partner's feelings, so we will explore these invisible signs as well.

Much of what *Love Signals* reports derives from field observations. After receiving my Ph.D. in anthropology from the University of Washington, I immersed myself in singles culture and watched as men and women fumbled to connect at parties, in coffeehouses, and in bars. Observing covertly from behind the potted palm, I became what French anthropologist Claude Lévi-Strauss has called the "alienated eye-witness." I found a universal pattern in the way couples related, nonverbally, beneath spoken words. Whether one lives in New Delhi, New Guinea, or New York, the same body language is used to attract a mate. In *Love Signals*, I will tell you what I have learned.

The study of body language is more scientific now than it has been in the past. In the 1960s, some viewed nonverbal communication as little more than a subjective branch of phrenology. Advances in neuroscience, evolutionary biology, and emotion research have made body language a scientifically credible field today. Researchers have mapped the precise neural pathways that link nonverbal signals to the nervous system. What this means for courtship is that you can read unspoken motives, emotions, and feelings with greater clarity and precision.

Love Signals is part ethnography and part how-to. It documents the little courting rituals you see in elevators, on subways, and in the workplace. It suggests ways to gaze, ways to read eyes across a room, and ways to sit, stand, align, walk, dress, and lift a drink to participate in the fascinating adventure of finding, winning, and keeping a mate. Knowing the unspoken vocabulary of love signals gives you an edge. The more you know about the nonverbal idiom of attraction, the more likely you will find a loving, lasting partner. Have fun observing, and enjoy the quest!

LOVE
SIGNALS

1. THE FIVE PHASES OF COURTSHIP

Once I'm done with kindergarten, I'm going to find me a wife.
—TOM (AGE 5)

It's better to be looked over than overlooked.
—MAE WEST

LOVE SIGNALS IS a practical field guide to the body language of courtship. It explores the nonverbal signs, signals, and cues human beings exchange to attract and keep their mates. As a medium of communication, love's silent language predates speech by millions of years. Indeed, humans wooed in a nonverbal idiom well before they could speak. And today, despite the world's estimated six thousand spoken languages, we still express emotions and feelings largely apart from words.

The first scientific study of courtship in our species, Homo sapiens, took place in the 1960s. Using a camera with mirror lenses to film couples without disturbing them, biologist Irenäus Eibl-Eibesfeldt of Germany's Max Planck Institute documented many of the common flirting rituals seen around the world. A student of Konrad Lorenz, Eibl-Eibesfeldt wrote his doctorate, "Breeding Biology of the Common Toad," before turning his lenses on human beings. From research in Brazil, Samoa, Paris, and other exotic field sites, Eibl-Eibesfeldt discovered a universal vocabulary of nonverbal signs used in seduction, flirtation, and courtship.

Since the 1960s, thousands of research projects in archaeology, biology, anthropology, linguistics, primatology, psychology, and psychiatry have been completed, establishing a virtual dictionary of courting cues. In the 1990s, we learned a great deal more about how the body speaks its mind apart from words. Progress made in neuroscience during the 1990–2000 Decade of the Brain and afterward has provided a clearer picture of what the unspoken signs in courtship's lexicon mean.

We now know more about how the brain processes nonverbal cues. Just as the brain's newer speech centers, for example, Broca's and Wernicke's areas, control language, older brain areas oversee communication apart from words. Specialized circuits of the central nervous system send, receive, and process speechless signs apart from our conscious awareness.

> We now know more about how the brain processes nonverbal cues.

For the 90 percent of us who are right-handed, areas of the right-brain cerebral hemisphere process nonverbal cues. Our right brain is more holistic, visuospatial, and intuitive than our left brain, which is more verbal, analytic, and rational than the right. A section in the middle of our brain called the *cingulate gyrus* produces nonverbal signs of emotion. We detect facial cues and hand gestures through dedicated layers of cerebral cortex located at the sides of our brain. Thanks to brain-and-behavior research, body language has come of age in the twenty-first century as a science to help us understand the hidden meanings of attraction, courtship, and love.

The Nonverbal Language of Love

Our unspoken language of love is universal. The postures, gestures, and facial cues of attraction are everywhere the same, in all societies and cultures. A case in point is the *en face* gaze. *En face* is an intimate form of eye-to-eye contact between mothers and newborns. An affectionate mother moves her face to within inches of her baby's face and positions her eyes in parallel alignment with her baby's eyes for optimal eye contact. Her *en face* gaze completely captivates the newborn, stops its crying, and nurtures a strong mother-child bond. Pediatricians view *en face* communication as a sort of "mating dance." Mother and child gaze in seeming rapture, synchronize their body movements, and imitate each other's facial expressions to enhance compatibility and build rapport.

En face is a worldwide courting ritual as well. Affectionate couples move their faces within inches of each other's face, lock eyes, and gaze deeply to show their love. Figuratively, they become each other's baby. A potent love signal, *en face* is as romantic and compelling in Alabama as it is in Zululand.

Since the body language of courtship is universal, you needn't speak the native tongue to attract a mate. One of the most exotic courtships I know of, between a tall, white, middle-aged New Jersey man and a short, teenage, African Pygmy, took place entirely apart from speaking. Before their engagement, neither she nor he uttered a mutually intelligible word. Gestures accomplished what conversation could not.

If the language of love is universal, you might wonder why we need a field guide to decipher its cues. One reason is that people postpone marriage in favor of careers today. As a result, they have problems attracting partners who are older, wiser, busier—and choosier. Thirty-somethings are less automatically smitten than they were as youths in high school. Another reason is that divorced men and women feel out of practice. They have trouble decoding the love signals they received earlier in their teens and twenties. Many, who avoided flirting after marriage, find it hard to shift gears and flirt again. In large metropolitan areas like Los Angeles, Chicago, and New York, thousands of eligible partners await the attention of complete strangers. In the past—in rural areas—people were more likely to court familiar folk who were known to be "safe." Unacquainted couples often had matchmakers to ease them through the psychological barrier of stranger anxiety.

The dating scene is different today. Urban singles find themselves surrounded by strangers. Some use video dating services, go on cruises, run personal ads in newspapers, or search the Internet. Many find that interacting with people who are unfamiliar can be uncomfortable, unpredictable, even unsafe. Is that woman sincere? Is she telling the truth? Can I trust this man? Is he genuine? Is he dangerous? What clues should I look for?

Answers to these questions lie not in words, which can be deceptively manipulated, but in more candid, unedited signs from our faces, bodies, and hands. Silent messages emitted from shoulder shrugs, eyeblinks, aftershaves, eyebrows, tattoos, and toe cleavage fill the nonverbal landscape *Love Signals* explores. Used as a field guide to the natural history of courtship, *Love Signals* shows how to read beneath and between a partner's spoken lines.

> Silent messages emitted from shoulder shrugs, eyeblinks, aftershaves, eyebrows, tattoos, and toe cleavage fill the nonverbal landscape *Love Signals* explores.

As you will see, the body's unspoken script reveals volumes about hidden agendas, feelings, and fears. Estimates of what percentage of our total communication is nonverbal range from 60 to 93 percent. In courtship, the percentage of emotional communication that is nonverbal exceeds 99 percent. When it comes to emotions, instead of verbalizing how we feel, our bodies do the talking.

What Do Hands Say?

A case in point is hands, which attract special notice in courtship. We find fingers, palms, and wrists incredibly appealing to look at. Dedicated centers in our temporal lobes, the cerebral lobes located just above our ears on either side of the brain, respond exclusively to hand shapes (Kandel, 1991). Both men and women are unconsciously alert to the physical appearance of each other's hands and digits as well as to their expressive shapes and gestures.

Showing an upraised open palm is universally friendly. Recognized around the world, this inviting hand gesture says, "You may approach."

In daily life and in art, hands are our "great communicators." Hands stand out in Michelangelo's sculpture of *David*, for example, and in his paintings on the Sistine Chapel ceiling. Hands establish the contemplative mood depicted in Rodin's masterpiece, *The Thinker*. Thanks to the temporal lobes, hands "speak" to us and attract almost as much notice as faces.

In courtship, palm-up gestures are psychologically friendlier than palm-down cues. The palm-up gesture is part of a submissive shoulder-shrug display identified by Charles Darwin in 1872 in his classic book *The Expression of the Emotions in Man and Animals*. Upraised palms are gestural remnants of an ancestral crouching posture, a primevally protective pose designed to be defensive rather than offensive. Neural roots of the protective crouch reach back at least five hundred million years.

Women find men's hands and wrists most attractive. In courtship, display them with rolled-up sleeves.

Holding a jacket slung over the shoulder displays the masculine forearm, wrist, and hand.

In courtship, palm-up gestures are psychologically friendlier than palm-down cues.

Our closest animal relatives, the chimpanzees, greet each other with compliant, upturned palms to show "I am friendly." For human beings everywhere, gesturing with an upraised, opened palm is a convincing and time-tested way to say "Trust me; I mean no harm." Throughout the world, palm-up cues captivate, charm, and psychologically disarm partners who may be unsure of each other's intentions.

In contrast, presenting a palm-down gesture is aggressive. Gesturing with the palm flipped downward as you speak, which is the pronated position a hand assumes in a push-up, is like slapping a desktop for emphasis. A palm-down hand cue resembles a sumo wrestler's ceremonial stomp in the ring. Since both gestures are assertive and emphatic, they are too forceful for courtship. Across the globe, palm-down gestures like striking a conference table to drive home a point are used to show authority and negative attitude.

An example is the widespread hand wag for "No!" in which a pronated palm wags back and forth to symbolize the human head shake of refusal. Another is the Greek "double-*moutza*" gesture in which both palms pronate and thrust horizontally outward to say "Go to hell twice." Aggressive, palm-down "beating" gestures make your ideas, opinions, and remarks more forceful as you speak, but they are decidedly unappealing in courtship.

At a wine-tasting party, I watched as friends Toni and Karen talked to strangers Bill and Steve. The foursome stood in a circle in the tasting room, holding wineglasses in their right hands. As Toni spoke, her left hand flipped upward to show an open palm. Holding her upper arm against the side of her body, she reached the open palm outward to Bill and Steve, seeming to draw them in with her hand. As Karen spoke, she held her wineglass in two hands. Karen rarely gestured, but when she did gesticulate she dropped her left hand to a position slightly below her wineglass, flipped her palm downward, and made choppy, up-and-down motions with her fingers stiffly extended. Karen's palm-down gestures added authority to her words but did not personally "connect" with the men.

Toni's palm-up gestures were frequent and friendly. Her left hand reached out and appealed for attention. Karen's gestures were sporadic, emphatic, and intense. A palm was nowhere to be seen, and her hand's jerky, batonlike motions made her seem less friendly and not as approachable. How did the men respond? Bill and Steve gave Toni noticeably more attention. They looked and smiled at her more, and head-nodded and gestured more—with palm-up cues of their own. In courtship, it goes without saying that hands make a difference.

Like the sumo wrestler's foot stomp, palm-down hand gestures are controlled subcortically by *basal ganglia*. The basal ganglia are primeval motor centers embedded in our brain's cerebral hemispheres that govern a reptilian display called the *high stand*. Like the iguana's push-up to seem "bigger" to rival males, our own palm-down gestures derive from the ancestral high-stand display. Down-turned palms are less attractive in courtship because they suggest power at the expense of friendliness. In the 1950s, Elvis Presley gestured with upturned palms to draw women near. The palm-down hand signals of today's rap singers seem to say "Get out of my face."

The Body Language of Strangers

Presenting a friendly, open palm is an effective way to break through courtship's *stranger barrier*. The stranger barrier evolved millions of years ago to protect us from being harmed by potentially dangerous, unknown human beings. Xenophobia (*xenos* is Greek for "stranger," and *phobos* for "fear") is a common human condition. Every culture mistrusts the stranger in its midst, and each of us experiences mild-to-moderate wariness around newcomers and outsiders—even those we find attractive.

In courtship, someone you have not properly met makes you feel uneasy and self-conscious. The anxious feeling is perfectly normal. Sixty years ago, psychologist Edward Thorndike proposed that the fear of strangers is innate. Later research confirmed that what psychologists call *stranger anxiety* is indeed a widespread—possibly universal—human response.

As a stranger approaches, your palms may turn cold as the sympathetic nervous system constricts blood vessels in your hands. Your level of blood adrenaline rises, and your palms sweat enough to register a galvanic-skin, or polygraph, response. For some, enough perspiration is released during courtship to make a friendly handshake too embarrassing.

Stranger anxiety starts in infancy, between five and nine months of age, along with a general apprehension of almost anything new. It is to our advantage to be cautious about picking up strange objects—or about being picked up by strange adults. Wariness protects us from harm.

Fear responses spontaneously emerge in monkeys between two and three months of age. At around six months, human babies begin to show such readable signs of wariness as crying, clinging, and gazing away to the side. Another wariness cue is a sudden, slight frown that creates vertical forehead wrinkles above the infant's nose. To pediatricians this telltale expression is known as *sobering*. Stranger wariness peaks around eighteen months and declines after age two or three.

Though it subsides in childhood, fear of strangers never fully goes away. Stranger anxiety runs especially high in courtship. It's what keeps you from asking someone you don't know out on a date. Nonverbally, stranger anxiety shows in gaze-aversion when a partner's eyes shift away from you to one side, in lip-biting mannerisms, and in tightly in-rolled or compressed lips.

Though it subsides in childhood, fear of strangers never fully goes away.

These are the same protective facial expressions infants give when a stranger looms too close for comfort. As adults, we unwittingly compress our lips, lip-bite, and turn our heads away to avoid eye contact in elevators with people we don't know—and with partners we've not yet met. We are not literally afraid of them, but wariness cues telegraph a reticence that suggests we are unwilling to meet. Though the signals may be fleeting, they register enough to keep us apart.

For successful first meetings in courtship, avoid stranger-anxiety cues. Since you are not aware of sending them, inadvertent gaze avoidance and tight lips are hard to control. Knowing what the signals look like—and what causes the body to "leak" them—can keep anxiety cues in check. Your face, neck, and shoulder muscles are controlled by special visceral nerves. When you feel the least bit anxious, emotional circuits automatically contract the muscles that produce aversive facial- and head-movement cues.

Tom, thirty-two, complained that women never talked to him in bars. Even when friends helped by attracting women to his table, the women eagerly chatted with everybody but Tom. They ignored him as if he were not there. A videotape of Tom seated in the barroom revealed why: Each time he made eye contact, Tom compressed his lips into a thin line. His tightened, in-rolled lips made him look unhappy and displeased. He was not angry, of course, but scared. Women who knew Tom described him as good-looking and sensitive, but the lip clench kept strangers away. Seeing himself on video enabled him to relax his mouth, and magically, solitude disappeared.

An Expression You Should Never Show

A stranger's presence prompts the brain's *amygdala,* a primitive arousal center located at the front of our temporal lobes, to produce the tensed jaws, tightened lips, and lowered eyebrows that signal unease about meeting someone new. The body's innate *freeze reaction* also may be touched off, causing postural immobility and an unsmiling—or "frozen"—face. The amygdala excites brain-stem circuits to activate these and other protective postures and facial expressions. Though you might like the nice-looking stranger to come a little closer, your face and body discourage the move with subtly discouraging messages that seem to say "Stay away."

Stranger anxiety may trigger an aversive facial expression called the *tongue show.* In tongue-showing, the tongue protrudes slightly and just the tip shows between the lips. The tongue show has been decoded as a socially negative sign in gorillas and human beings. A gorilla pushed from his favorite seat on a log, or a man entering a roomful of strangers, unwittingly shows the tongue in "displeasure." The tongue show, a defensive sign children use when approaching strange adults, has been deciphered by researchers as an antisocial cue that means "Don't bother me."

The brain's amygdalae can prompt clearly visible negative signals in courtship.

Seeing a tongue show, clenched jaw, or furrowed brow may keep you from approaching someone new at a party. You may suppose she finds you unattractive or imagine he finds something eccentric about your ankle tattoo. Understanding the psychology of stranger anxiety should reassure you that an unwilling face says little about you personally. At the very beginning of a relationship, your partner knows nothing about you. Your only fault is that you are momentarily a stranger, and this fact alone should not keep you from moving closer.

Get Closer with the Familiarity Effect

Studies in Korea, Japan, and the United States reveal that even slight familiarity with a stranger can lead to greater feelings of attraction and liking. Knowing where she works or where he worships can add a comforting level of predictability and safeness. In courtship, the simplest way to become more familiar is through a nonverbal technique called *mere exposure*. First reported by psychologist Robert Zajonc in 1968, mere exposure, also known as the *familiarity effect*, is the principle that repeated exposure to almost any stimulus—an oil painting, a Chinese ideogram, or a stranger—can arouse subliminally positive feelings of "liking" for that stimulus (Zajonc, 1968). Simply put, mere exposure is the idea that you like someone you've already seen better than someone who is unfamiliar.

In courtship, mere exposure works even in impersonal spaces like elevators. When you ride the same elevator to work each day, you develop an emotional kinship with those you usually see. You may smile, nod your head, and lift your eyebrows in recognition. You may say "Good morning," but speech is not required for mere exposure to work. From studies of how human relationships emerge and take form, psychologists have learned that physical proximity itself is the key. Researchers conclude that the closer your functional distance, that is, the more times you sit near him in a cafeteria or bump into her on an elevator, the closer you both will feel. From mere exposure alone, you are liable to like— and be liked by—the person who is emotionally "closer" than others who work just down the hall but who rarely cross your path.

The principle of mere exposure is predictability and safeness. The human brain prefers what is known to that which is unknown. In his experiments, Zajonc showed Chinese written characters, or ideograms, to subjects who had no understanding of Chinese. Later, he showed them novel Chinese characters, but his subjects liked the original ones better—simply because they were familiar. Mere exposure to the initially presented symbols was enough to set a preference.

> The human brain prefers what is known to what is unknown.

Zajonc's familiarity principle is especially valid for faces. We strongly prefer faces we know to those we do not recognize. The principle holds even for subtle facial details. In a classic study, researchers showed women two photographs of themselves (Mita, Dermer, and Knight, 1977). One photo was of the face taken normally, as a true camera image, while the second was taken as a mirror image with reversed right and left sides. Because of slight asymmetries in its features, the two halves of a human face do not perfectly match. Predictably, women in the study liked the reversed-image photos of themselves better since these compared with what they saw everyday in the mirror. Their friends preferred the true-image photos because these matched how they saw their classmates everyday in the flesh.

Applied to courtship, mere exposure suggests that before speaking to an unfamiliar man or woman you establish a baseline of familiarity. This prepares the partner by laying psychological groundwork in which a new relationship can germinate. Before you ask the nice-looking Safeway clerk for a date, go through the clerk's checkout line to build familiarity. Establish eye contact, smile, bow your head forward, head-nod in agreement, and show an open palm. Three visits in as many days activates the familiarity effect. The odds that he or she will agree to take an espresso break with you dramatically improve. Repeated physical proximity over short periods of time converts you from "just a stranger" to someone who is better known and "liked."

Attracting with Your Eyebrows

An appealing way to greet someone new is with a universal sign biologists call the *eyebrow flash of recognition*. This cue is decoded everywhere as a sign of friendship and goodwill. You make eye contact, smile, lift both eyebrows, and briefly glance away. The eyebrow raise is a positive signal that says "I'm happy to see you." Gazing away suggests you expect nothing in return. When combined, the two eye messages make your greeting emotionally unconditional. You neither pressure nor wait for a response in kind.

As your face becomes familiar, your persona is better liked. Zajonc thinks the mere-exposure effect is deeply rooted in our species' evolutionary psychology. It is probable that our earliest hominid ancestors considered familiar males and females safer than those who were strange. The rule of repeated exposure affects how we relate to potential mates today. In its own evolution, courtship has been uniquely crafted to familiarize.

What Is Courtship?

The word *courtship* evolved from the seven-thousand-year-old Indo-European root *gher-*, which means "to grasp or enclose." In every culture, human beings attain the closeness of sexual intimacy through courtship, a usually slow negotiation based on exchanges of nonverbal signals and words. Since vertebrates from reptiles to primates reproduce by mating and internal fertilization of the female's body, couples must get physically close enough to touch. Through its five phases, human courtship is the means by which two people close the physical gap—and the emotional distance separating them—to become a loving pair.

> Courtship itself is peculiar in being the preliminary to another activity—mating.
>
> —Margaret Bastock

In his book *The Naked Ape*, biologist Desmond Morris calls humans the "sexiest" primates. Monkeys and most apes breed seasonally, sometimes for just a few weeks each year, but humans can make love in any season and at any stage of the female's monthly cycle. Men and women have made love in trees, aboard airplanes, and on the steps of the U.S. Capitol—virtually anyplace and everyplace, including outer space. Though inquiries on the subject are discouraged, NASA doesn't deny that sexual activity has taken place in orbit.

Anytime, anyplace—but not with anyone. We are more fastidious about partners than we are about time and space. We pick and choose. The selection process is courtship. Most of us identify courtship only with attracting a mate, but it has an equally important repelling side. Courtship attracts and repulses, says yes *and* no. It is a double-edged sword that rules in and rules out.

An apt analogy is that of a screen. Courtship is like a sieve that separates coarse from fine. It chooses and refuses but especially the latter, because courtship keeps out more people than it lets in. Most courtships end in screen-out several stages before intimacy.

At its heart, courtship is a dialogue about personal proximity and physical closeness. It runs on messages—on tangible signals and visible displays. Love itself is an intangible, but love communication is concrete. Before we love, we exchange come-hither messages granting permission to approach. A man tilts his head sideward like a little boy; a woman responds with a coy lifting of her shoulders.

The Cheyenne Indians of the Great Plains are a case in point. In the 1850s, a Cheyenne brave stood silently, with his head lowered, alongside a maiden's usual footpath and timidly waited. As the maiden passed by, the young man froze, statuelike, until she gave a faint signal recognizing his presence: a brief smile, perhaps, or a quick look up from under her eyebrows. The brave's courage would build, and the next time she walked by he might gently tug on her skirt (Hoebel, 1978). Cheyenne courtship started as loving relationships begin everywhere—slowly, tentatively, and silently.

The Five Phases of Courtship

As a nonverbal process, courtship moves slowly through five distinct phases. Worldwide, the stages are the same: (1) Attention, (2) Recognition, (3) Speech, (4) Touching, and (5) Lovemaking. Each phase has its own signs, signals, and cues. Since potential mates "test" each other before uniting as one, courtship is rarely hurried. Moving too fast—giving too many signals at once or showing them out of phase order—may frighten a partner away. Universally, patience is the key. A pair bond gradually forms through a choreographed give-and-take of signs granting physical and emotional closeness.

PHASE ONE: ATTRACTING ATTENTION. In the first or *Attention Phase* of courtship, people beam out signals to announce "I am here" and "I am female" (or "male"). With their clothing, facial adornment, aromas, gestures, and deeds, nonverbal messages are broadcast in all directions to attract notice, well before words are exchanged. At the same time, *threat-disclaiming* cues suggest "I mean you no harm." Charles Darwin called these harmless signals *submissive displays*.

We broadcast hundreds of beckoning messages, from the decrescendo laugh a woman gives to announce her presence at a party to the diffident, pigeon-toed posture a man shyly assumes to invite approach. In the chapters that follow, I will decode these nonverbal bids for attention much as anthropologists decipher hidden meanings in drum signals, picture writing, whistle languages, and dance.

SHOW NO HARM

For some animals, sending the right signals in courtship is a matter of life or death. Consider the wolf spider, who must get near enough to his grumpy mate to insert a sperm packet into her body. One too-eager footstep as he creeps down her earthen burrow and she attacks him, imagining he is either a predator or prey. Male wolf spiders must approach slowly, because the slowed motion is a cue: "I mean no harm." When he meets her head-on in the dark, he must reach out and stroke her body gently, in just the right way, or she kills him on the spot.

The psychology of spider courtship is not unlike that of humans. Should a man blindside a woman in a singles' bar—approach her suddenly without bowing his body forward, tilting his head, lifting his shoulders submissively, and extending an open palm—her body language may tell him (figuratively, of course) to drop dead. She will tense her lips and swivel around on her barstool, turn her face and body completely away, and give him a "cold shoulder." In the courtship of humans and animals, we should not underestimate the power of Charles Darwin's submissive displays.

PHASE TWO: ATTRACTING ATTENTION or reading the gleam in an eye. The *Recognition Phase*, like a bat's sonar, begins as you seek nonverbal responses to signs emitted in the Attention Phase. "I am here! I am female! . . . Do you see me?" Recognition cues give information about having been noticed. They are the incoming signs received in response to outgoing cues previously sent. A woman tests a man's reaction to her physical presence by reaching around him for hors d'oeuvres on an appetizer tray. Should he lift his shoulders, tilt his head, and smile, his body language says that he likes being near her. On the other hand, a deadpan "blank face" and angling his body away telegraph indifference—or say that she is "too close for comfort." Recognition cues show where you stand in a relationship before you say hello. More important, they reveal who you should say hello *to*.

PHASE THREE: EXCHANGING WORDS or what to say and how to say it. From nonverbal cues advertising presence, gender, and safeness, you move to courtship's third or *Conversation Phase*. Signs exchanged in the previous phases enable couples to penetrate the unseen barrier of stranger anxiety. So hindering is this invisible wall of suspicion that many would-be pairs never get beyond posturing to conversation. Men and women who are strongly drawn to each other may be unable to connect in words for months, even years.

Some think you shouldn't talk to strangers without having something witty or important to say. Remember that courtship is 99 percent nonverbal. What is said matters less than the saying. Research on opening lines shows that "Hello" works most of the time for men and all of the time for women. Of course, social psychologists who do the research don't consider the preparatory gestures needed to spark a conversation in the first place. *Love Signals* decodes these prefacing cues and shows how lip, eye, brow, face, head, shoulder, arm, hand, and finger movements help or hinder your spoken remarks. At the close quarters of speaking face-to-face, nonverbal signs of liking, trust, deceit, and willingness to commit are available for the reading.

FIELD NOTES:
THE CASE OF THE CAFETERIA COURTSHIP

"Friday P.M., Oct. 8—On the University of Washington campus, cool, light rain," my field notes read. No one was sitting on the damp, spongy lawn outside, so it was time to move the observations indoors. The lunch crowd in the cafeteria had thinned to one or two persons per table in the huge dining hall. Stranger anxiety leads college students to spread out and occupy vacant tables whenever they can.

I sat and kept my eyes on a cluster of tables, each occupied by a lone man or woman. I nibbled on a hamburger to reassure those around me that I was safe. In her studies, primatologist Dian Fossey chewed on tropical leaves and belched audibly to calm skittish mountain gorillas in Rwanda. Eating together shows animals you mean no harm. If it worked with apes, the behavior would work with students.

The strategy paid off. Halfway through my Huskyburger, I saw a graduate student, a scholarly type—beard, khaki pants, and tweed jacket—put his food tray on the far corner of a co-ed's table. The young woman had a scholarly look, too. She wore black tights, no makeup, her hair in a bun. I sensed attraction because he tossed his head after glancing at her. The quick *head toss*, to flip wayward bangs from his forehead, revealed a brain stem engaged in arousal. If unaffected by her presence, he wouldn't have tossed his head.

The courtship began slowly—and cautiously—like others I had seen. Around the world, in people and animals, courtship calls for unhurried approaches to keep mates from attacking or running away.

Watching the vignette unfold, I note how each person studiously ignores the other until she, not he, tenders the first beckoning cue. The woman takes an art book from her bag, sets it down with a thump on the table, and angles her upper body toward his. Without looking at him, she conspicuously thumbs pages to draw his attention. The man, in turn, without gazing at the woman's face or eyes, slowly shifts his weight and brings his shoulders into alignment with hers. Anthropologists call mirroring of this sort *postural echo*. Finally, in a conscious act of will, he breaks through the invisible force-field of her presence to gaze down at her opened book. Not at her directly, not yet, but now they have an all-important *shared focus*. Instead of relating to each other, one-on-one, they relate indirectly—and less threateningly—through the art book.

Seconds after looking at her book, the young man stretches, raises fisted hands to shoulder level, spreads his elbows widely, yawns, and thrusts out his chest. Mirroring his action, she stretches and returns the chest protrusion, and their eyes finally meet. After a period of nonverbal posturing, eye-to-eye contact is established at last. Twenty minutes later, the two are smiling, head-nodding, and flexing their shoulders in tandem as they speak. "Doing the same thing," known to anthropologists as *isopraxism*, strengthens the burgeoning bond. After being together for thirty minutes, they say good-bye—but not before trading phone numbers on pieces of scrap paper. The couple passed through courtship's first three stages in just half an hour.

PHASE FOUR: THE LANGUAGE OF TOUCH. The *Touching Phase* begins with the first tactile contact, from an "accidental" knee-brushing beneath a table to a more deliberate tap on the shoulders or back. After smell, touch is humankind's oldest sense. So powerful are touch cues that initial body contact must be made with care. In a restaurant, if a man stretches an arm toward his date across the tabletop, she might read his casual reach as an invitation to touch. As a test, the woman should place her fingertips on his forearm and say something like "I'm glad we came here." This allows her to read his willingness to be touched before trying a more serious handhold after the meal. Does he startle and pull away from her tap? He may not be ready for courtship's tactile stage. If he relaxes, leans in, and touches her hand, they successfully enter Phase Four.

PHASE FIVE: MAKING LOVE. When partners receive tactile reassurance from each other, lovemaking may follow. The most intimate stage of courtship is, like the phases before it, replete with nonverbal cues. Embraces, pats, *en face* gazes, snuggles, nuzzles, cuddles, and kisses prevail as couples care for, handle, and treat each other tenderly as babies. Sexually, the most effective touch zones in Phase Five are thighs, derriere, and the "saddle" area. Anatomists call the latter region *sexual skin*. Touching in these zones stimulates nerve endings allied with the *pudendal nerve*, which prepares the sexual organs for duty on our species' behalf.

Voice contact continues. Couples exchange words in softer, higher-pitched voices. Physically through sound, words caress as gently and persuasively as fingertips. Our early amphibian ancestors "heard" vibrations conducted as tactile signals through the lower jaw. Millions of years later these perceptive jaw bones became the malleus, incus, and stapes of the inner ears. Our brain still responds to love talk as an intimate form of "touching."

After making love, courtship wanes as couples trade fewer wooing cues. Some say the relationship loses its "magic," but a better reason is that after negotiating intimate closeness, the pair need not renegotiate with quite the same ardor. Since nearness is not the problem it originally was, fewer signals need be exchanged to attain it. Taking proximity for granted makes the body language of lovers noticeably calmer than that of couples who have not made love.

. . .

IN COURTSHIP, KNOWLEDGE is power. Knowing that gestures work better than words gives you a clear advantage in finding a mate. Nonverbal signals rouse deeper parts of the emotional brain, where mating instincts lie. Facial expressions, body movements, and postures register with more immediacy than do the linguistic sounds of speech. As world travelers know, you needn't speak the native tongue to flirt.

2. PHASE ONE: ATTRACTING ATTENTION

He slowly circles her, making an occasional bow
in front of her until she solicits.
—MARGARET BASTOCK
(ON THE COURTSHIP OF THE BLACK GROUSE)

K NOWING HOW TO "advertise" is the first step on courtship's five-fold path. The Attention Phase can be anxiety ridden because your persona, self-image, and body movements go on display. Men show off for women, and women show off for men. Gender advertisements in hairdos, footwear, and clothing range from mild-mannered to pointedly bold. A man may wear his favorite T-shirt or an Armani suit to accent the strength of his masculine frame. A woman may wear a plain beige top or a red dress with puffy sleeves to accentuate the friendliness—and approachability—of lifted shoulders. The choices are vast, the messages are the same.

Attention Phase cues advertise physical presence, gender, and friendly intentions. Bright colors, bold contrasts, and conspicuous gestures say, "I am here." Gender is displayed in a man's wider shoulders, larger jaw, and deeper voice, each of which says, "I am male." Narrower shoulders, a smaller chin, and a lighter voice say, "I am female." For both sexes, deferential shoulder shrugs, side-tilted heads, and bared throats say, "I am harmless; you may approach."

The best strategy in courtship is to attract notice without seeming too obvious, eager, or blunt in the process. Overstatements in Phase

One—coming on too colorfully, too aromatically, or too soon—keep others away. Courtship works on a principle of luring. Instead of chasing, cornering, and capturing a mate, you emit "come hither" signals and await a response. You hold back initially and play what amounts to a waiting game, in which lure, not seize, is the rule.

FIELD NOTES: RESTLESS IN SEATTLE

Welcome to Monkeyshines, an Irish-theme establishment for singles in Seattle, complete with wood paneling, brass rails, and overhanging ivy. A conspicuous twenty-five-year-old man, whom we shall nickname "Leather Vest," wants to meet a woman at Monkeyshines. Leather Vest makes many common mistakes of men who seem too eager to make contact. His demeanor, which attracts too much attention, keeps women away.

Leather Vest swaggers into Monkeyshines and with a flurry of gestures claims a small round table near the bar's front window. With a flick of his wrist, he tosses a cigarette pack on the tabletop and then picks the pack up and takes out a Camel. Vest drums the cigarette on his thumb, involving his whole upper body in the tapping motion. After lighting the cigarette, he wags the match out with a flourish, and exhales a conspicuous cannon burst of smoke. Without so much as a word, he drives the point home: "I am here."

But Leather Vest is here by himself. As a lone male, his presence seems a little suspect, and few females gaze his way. He has on a brown plaid shirt, open at the neck, and form-fitting denim jeans. A tiny red label situated high on his right buttock calls attention to his bottom. The crisscrossing lines of his shirt catch the eye, as does the contrasting centerpiece of his outfit, a shiny, chocolate-brown cowhide vest.

Constantly in motion—changing position, shifting his weight, and moving his hands—Vest restlessly works his lure, but women stay away. Impatient, he does an about-face and leans back against the tabletop, resting his elbows behind him on the marble. He gazes in annoyance with a curled upper lip at the men seated behind the bar, as if challenging them to look back.

When his Tequila Sunset arrives, he keeps his wrist rigid and uses his whole arm to stir the drink. He lifts it to his mouth as if curling a barbell. He head-tosses to clear his bangs, conspicuously smokes another cigarette, sits down, stands up, turns around, and nervously stretches his arms. Vest alternately stands and sits in his strutting ground, like a sage grouse, gesturing for all to see. His every movement has some body English or curlicue added. He lures but with too much emphasis, and no women come near.

On analysis, Leather Vest's Attention Phase signaling is off by a third. He is fine on two points: he lets people know (1) that he is present, and (2) that he is a male. These messages are clear, but his act completely misses on the essential third point. Vest does not let women know he is "vulnerable," which is to say, he gives no visible signs of harmlessness. He is a lone stranger showing too much attitude for comfort.

Leather Vest should counterbalance his assertive stance with softer cues. Instead of staring around the room with his head tipped backward, disdainfully peering down his nose, he should gaze with his head tipped slightly forward. Using the more submissive, bowed-head position—a subtle posture suggesting "sensitivity"—Vest could establish a friendlier, more disarming presence.

To seem more approachable, Vest might use a diffident, self-touching gesture such as clasping the front of his neck with his fingertips. The neck touch, an unconscious sign of insecurity, would disclose that he is not totally self-assured. A clumsy mannerism like dropping his cigarette would show he is accessible and not likely to pounce should a female come near. Even his courting territory, the small round table for three, is too personal for a woman to approach without making a statement. Invading Vest's exclusive domain would be a too-frank admission of interest. He should establish his presence at one of the roomier, more sociable tables where women could approach without giving themselves away.

No alternative to the macho-cowboy guise was presented. After an hour of posturing like a lion—but with no takers—Leather Vest left the bar like a lamb. Had his animal psychology been reversed, he might have emerged from Monkeyshines with a partner by his side.

The Unwritten Rules of Luring

From a peacock's iridescent tail feathers to a gypsy moth's irresistible scent, the courtship of animals has much to teach us about luring a mate. The stunningly colorful, precoital display of the male peacock is enough to entice even an unacquainted female to mate on the spot. So strong is the gypsy moth's aromatic "disparlure," a word that combines the insect's species name, *dispar*, with *lure*, that a single molecule of the female's scent can be picked up by a male hovering seven miles away.

Shorter-distance luring accounts for much of what goes on at parties, dance clubs, and singles' bars. The scene at Seattle's Monkeyshines is a case in point. On Friday nights, the twenty-five- to forty-year-old professionals in business garb come to Monkeyshines to see and be seen. Voices boil up in the crowd as visitors drink piña coladas beneath wicker-and-walnut–bladed fans and tear-drop ceiling lights. Enthusiastic greetings, earnest small talk, and overzealous laughter—a constant, droning loudness—fills the space. At first the noise is upsetting, but after a glass of your favorite beverage, you relax, and watch Attention-Phase cues seeming to ricochet off the walls.

At three marble-topped tables in the middle of the bar, we see solitary men standing and drinking at respectful distances from one another. As competitors in courtship, they say nothing to their fellow males. Instead, they stand there silently, as strangers, drinking and watching—and posturing.

The unpaired men here week after week are the regulars at Monkeyshines. Aggressively costumed in jackets and ties, they work the passive lure. Each man expects that on the strength of his appearance, physical charm, and clothing—on his stance, the way he leans, and the engaging way he looks around as he sips a beer—that he might attract an available female to come and drink at his table. Not drink and talk, not yet, just drink and stand near at first so he might send short-distance cues that could lead to talking.

The Bowerbird's Lure

To a biologist studying the courtship of birds, the weekly ritual of Monkeyshines' regulars would resemble the luring technique of an Australian fowl called the satin bowerbird. The black, robin-size male builds a ground nest of thin sticks designed to lure mates closer. About twelve inches high and open at both ends, the nest looks like a corridor or a stall. By itself on the sand, his nest is no more impressive than two clumps of bunch grass. So the bird adds a twig porch which he decorates with snail shells, pebbles, blossoms, and feathers, and if near a town, with cast-off plastic buttons, pieces of glass, marbles, and tin lids. With its gaudy front porch, a bowerbird's nest is so attractive to the females that one will walk into the bower on her own. She will stand in the twig corridor facing the display of odd objects, and then courtship will shift into its second stage.

The regular males at Monkeyshines behave like bowerbirds. First, each man establishes a fixed courting space that is his and his alone. Second, each decorates the claimed spot with eye-catching artifacts: a conspicuous wallet, an expensive pen, a cell phone, car keys, a paperback novel, a notebook, a pile of cash and shiny silver coins. Along with the artifact scatter, his fashionably bedecked body is also on display. The point of the Attention Phase for men is to beam out attracting messages like those of the bowerbird. Monkeyshines' men display an area that extends from eighteen to forty-eight inches in front of the body to lure mates into their "personal zone." From this distance, face, eye, and gestural cues transmit most clearly and persuasively.

A woman who understands the attractiveness of her movements takes center stage without saying a word.

Unlike the males, Monkeyshines' females do not mark their tabletops. They keep possessions in purses and instead carry bags, contained and stowed out of sight. Stowage frees women to go on walkabout, to be more expressively mobile in the courting space. Since they do not claim fixed territories, females are freer to come and go, to promenade as they please, and to approach from strategic angles. In courtship, a woman who understands the attractiveness of her movements takes center stage without saying a word.

Two Are More Attractive Than One

As we watch, two women in their mid-twenties enter Monkeyshines through the shamrock-green front door. Single file, they negotiate the crowded, knee-brushing space of the foyer and walk on, past the tables occupied by solitary men. The women take stools at one end of a table for six, inhabited by a lone man working a crossword puzzle and nursing a Guinness. As they sit down, they speak in animated tones and then, without looking at him, because they are focused on each other, they emit a volley of Attention Phase cues.

The brunette head-tosses, jerking her head upward to sweep bangs higher off her eyebrows. The repeated hair-flipping calls attention to her face. In tandem, her blond friend periodically tilts her face upward, shakes her head, and with stiffened fingers trains long tresses over her ears and backward off her cheeks. Biologists recognize preening as a key behavior in the courtship of primates and birds. The young woman's preening brings notice to her well-groomed, shiny hair, which, in primates, is a sign of status, fitness, and good health.

With clearly visible cues, both women establish the fact that they are present and female. And with a darting glance, the man looks their way, but just as quickly returns his eyes to the crossword. Seemingly engrossed in words, he pretends not to see and yet definitely notices: "They are here."

Calling attention to one's face with hand, head, and hair movements is most effective when the facial features are animated with expressions.

Calling attention to one's face with hand, head, and hair movements is most effective when the facial features are animated with expressions. Eye-tracking research confirms that we notice speaking lips more than lips at rest. Studies find that an immobile face in repose—a deadpan face—is perceived as unreceptive, even unfriendly. At Crossword Puzzle's table, the women smile and part their lips as they speak. They head-nod in synchrony, lift their eyebrows in unison, and widen their eyes in concert. As a duo, their faces come alive, which makes them more engaging to watch than a crossword puzzle grid.

Luring as a team is better than luring alone.

In courtship, luring as a team is more effective than luring alone. Together in pairs, women at Monkeyshines give off emotional gestures, movements, and expressions that the solitary men, acting alone, cannot show. As they speak, the females flex and lift their shoulders, tilt their heads, and display friendly opened palms. Their bodies communicate energy, sociability, and presence. Beckoning from behind his artifact scatter, a male's body language is almost muted. Not only is he tethered to the tabletop, his face, hands, and shoulders have little to say. Though the bowerbird's lure is a decent start, he needs something livelier to suggest "I am here."

Showing Presence—"I Am Here"

For man and beast, establishing presence tops the agenda of courtship's Attention Phase. In the southeastern United States, a green anole lizard bobs his head, makes bowing movements, and exhibits his red dewlap to attract a mate. On the Midwestern plains, a prairie chicken leans forward, drops his wings, fans out his tail feathers, and inflates reddish-purple sacs on his neck to attract a hen. He struts about his courting territory, makes acrobatic aerial leaps, cackles, and gives a "booming" call that can be heard a mile away.

> Without conscious intent, we animate our hand gestures, kinetically move our heads, touch our own body—scratch, clasp, and massage ourselves to release pent-up energy—and walk faster than we would normally stroll at home.

We, like lizards and prairie chickens, rely on nonverbal signs to announce presence in courtship. At a party, loud music, loud greetings, and loud laughter proclaim the message "We are here!" Without conscious intent, we animate our hand gestures, kinetically move our heads, touch our own body—scratch, clasp, and massage ourselves to release pent-up energy—and walk faster than we would normally stroll at home. Each of these unpremeditated body movements announces our presence on courtship's crowded stage.

FIELD NOTES: THEY'VE GOT RHYTHM

Nowhere is the Phase One message "I am here" proclaimed more boisterously than on Greek Row. There is no better lab in which to study the mating dance. Each spring as chestnut trees leaf out and rhododendrons bloom in fraternity-house yards, extremely amplified rock music booms out of dormer windows and off roofs. Loud music, like birdsong, attracts attention and warns rival males that the space bordered by "our sound" is claimed.

We alert to rock's "big-seeming" sounds automatically—without conscious deliberation—because our brain's acoustical orienting response is subcortical. Our innate sense of sound detection is housed below the thinking forebrain, in ancient modules of the amphibian midbrain's *inferior colliculi*. In a courtship setting, music effectively links our minds and joins our bodies with its beat. Sharing the rhythm puts us on the same psychological wavelength and makes us feel more together.

On Greek Row in spring, the driveways, sidewalks, and front lawns come alive with moving bodies. To enhance visibility, young men and women walk, jog, and sprint from here to there—to almost anywhere at all—to catch each other's eyes. They spend a lot of time being outside and underway without having a fixed destination. The Greeks, like anole lizards and prairie chickens, understand at an intuitive level that motion catches the eye.

Since eyes are attracted to moving bodies, a man or woman in a fixed position is less likely to be noticed.

Just as ears orient to attention-grabbing sounds, eyes orient to movements. Eye-tracking studies show that our gaze zooms in on things that move. Since eyes are attracted to moving bodies, a man or woman in a fixed position is less likely to be noticed. Our innate sense of motion detection is housed below consciousness in midbrain vision centers called *superior colliculi*. The reflexive orientation of these centers to movement makes a body in motion incredibly more noticeable than an unmoving body in a chair. Moving for movement's sake—dancing, chasing a Frisbee, or simply jumping up and down in a volleyball game—is the worldwide norm in courtship. Greek Row clearly illustrates the fact that the human mating dance is literally that—a dance.

Rhythmic repetition is a common theme in animal courtship. Sight, hearing, and touch receptors pick up regularly repeated, rhythmic signals better than signals that are steady-state, static, or unchanging (Bastock, 1967). The zigzag dance of a male stickleback fish, the rhythmic chirping of a male cricket, and the pressure-sensitive waves emitted by undulating fish are well known in biology as attention-getting signs. In human courtship, the repetitive motions, sounds, and tactile sensations we emit while dribbling a ball, shooting baskets, or tossing footballs communicate the same message: "I am here."

How to Make a Silent Pass

A good way to be noticed at a party is to use an option called the *pass-by*. The pass-by resembles a well-known mating ritual of the stickleback fish, called the *zigzag dance*, in which males attract notice by approaching females and circling back across their field of view. In the pass-by, you walk directly in front of a targeted person, to within arm's reach, on your way to somewhere else. For decades, savvy women have gone out of their way en route to the ladies' room to walk past favored men. Countless alternate routes serve, including trips to the kitchen, the beverage cooler, the fireplace, or the patio. Destination is not the endpoint, only a means to be seen.

For the pass-by to work, pre-positioning is key. You take a position in which the viewer stands between yourself and the goal. Then, as Thoreau said, you walk confidently in the direction of your dreams. The procedure can be repeated to ensure your movements catch the stranger's eye. With proper nonchalance, a pass-by enables you to come physically near, to establish eye contact, and to take a visual reading of the partner's response to your closeness. Seeing lifted eyebrows, a head nod, a head tilt, a smile, or a longer-than-normal returned gaze of two to three seconds means you have established contact.

In his book *Silent Messages*, psychologist Albert Mehrabian notes that handkerchief-dropping "has long been universally recognized" as an attention-getting cue (1981:156). Though the handkerchief itself is obsolete, the principle of dropping things remains a viable option in courtship. Flirting consultants claim that the dropping ploy hardly ever fails, because the clumsy maneuver is a nonverbal appeal for help. More precisely, it is a submissive sign of "helplessness." From your pass-by route, you need only make eye contact, smile, and drop a party napkin. As the stranger bends down to help you pick it up, an opportunity for talking is proffered. Bowing down together sends a message of harmlessness that enables you to make a pass without actually "making a pass."

Zoologist Frans de Waal observed object-dropping in the courtship of our closest animal relative, the bonobo chimpanzee. A male named Mituo passed by Miso, a female, to climb higher in her tree. From his position above Miso, Mituo proceeded to drop broken twigs one by one. After several fell to the ground, each narrowly missing her, he silently swayed in the branches and dropped a few more. After four minutes, Miso ascended to meet excited Mituo, presented her hindquarters to him as a receptive sign, and copulation took place. Bonobo courtship is faster than our own, but dropping objects to gain attention is much the same: "Notice me: I am here."

Make a Fashion Statement

Like body movements, postures, and dropped objects, clothing is especially appealing to our visual sense. For men and women alike, brightly colored, high-contrast clothing worn on top is as perfectly adapted to gaining attention as the peacock's tail. In the Attention Phase, shirts, blouses, vests, and sweaters that stand out are better choices than tops in muted brown, olive, beige, gray, or "griege" worn in public areas, dance clubs, and bars.

Despite the popularity of black, our primate brain finds colorful hues—fruity ones in particular—more exciting to behold. Black shows presence and makes a serious fashion statement, but doesn't invite approach. Bright colors arouse emotions while darker shades hide and dampen them, much as sunglasses mask feelings revealed in eyes. According to neuroscientist Vilayanur Ramachandran, our brain delights in intensely exaggerated hues like the brilliant, saturated yellows of Van Gogh's sunflowers. Bright colors invite contact, because our primate eyes' *trichromatic* color sense evolved for fruit detection. In short, we notice fruity hues that are subliminally "edible."

Edge receptors in vision centers of the forebrain alert to lines, markings, insignia, patterns, labels, seals, banners, badges, symbols, spangles, and pins added to clothing. Their encoded messages provide information, rather than durability or function, and "speak" to us as gestures. In courtship, the linear detail and geometric design of a message T-shirt draw more attention than an unmarked T-shirt. Clothing asymmetries—a diagonal stripe, a lapel pin, or an insignia worn on one side of the body only—attract notice because they contrast with the bilateral symmetry of our upright, bipedal form. Asymmetries on so symmetrical a body jump out and catch eyes because the unusual is more intriguing than the norm.

In hairstyles, an asymmetrical part on one side makes your face more intriguing to look at than a part straight down the middle.

Do First Impressions Count?

Are first impressions transitory or lasting? Evidence supports the latter, according to University of Arizona communications professor Judee Burgoon. The initial reaction and sentiments we have when seeing someone for the first time generally persist after we meet the new person. What we originally notice sticks in memory, even when subsequent actions and body language contradict the first impression. However, Burgoon notes that physical attractiveness, which can be critical in first meetings, becomes less important as time goes by. After seeing a face several times, we admire its features more as the "familiarity effect" takes hold.

Message Hair. Whether it is wispy and short or soft and long, women's hair cries for attention in courtship. Bangs bring eyes to the face when hair color contrasts with the skin's lighter or darker tones. Today, few women wear "big hair," because it attracts too much attention and violates the safeness rule. Big hair is simply too big, and makes a head loom too close for comfort. It sends a message that the wearer wants too much attention. When beauticians for the movie *Steel Magnolias* (1989) tried to tone down Dolly Parton's big hair, she told them, "Heck, there's a big, crazy, larger-than-life personality in here" (Parton, 1994:277). Like the hair on her head, Dolly's message is clear.

With hairstyles, the only constant is change. Upper-class women in ancient Egypt wore giant wigs bedecked with colorful ribbons and jewelry to attract attention, as did French royal ladies thousands of years later in Marie Antoinette's court (Barber, 1994). Should big hair stage a comeback in courtship, as it no doubt will, the message will be the same: "I am here!"

Showing Gender—"I Am Male (or Female)"

As you establish physical presence in courtship, you simultaneously announce your sexual identity with gender cues. The sheer power of gender messages shows when men and women adopt each other's signals to "pass" as members of the opposite sex. There are documented cases of a woman passing as a man and marrying a woman, and of a man sleeping with another man he mistakenly thought to be female. Though it is common in certain fish for true females to turn into true males, and vice versa—for example, *Trimma okinawwae*, a variant of the gobi—it is not possible for humans to switch without surgical intervention. Gender signals may change in courtship, but sexual identity stays the same.

In the case of Spokane jazz musician Billy Tipton, "he" (really a she) masqueraded as a man for fifty years, married five times, adopted three sons, and became a scoutmaster and Little League coach. When Billy died in 1989 at age seventy-four, a coroner discovered his true sex and utterly shocked Tipton's family. So persuasive were his counterfeit gender cues that not one of the wives he courted, lived with, and made love to claimed to know Tipton was not really a man. On the other side of the gender coin is the celebrated case of a Japanese man who passed as a woman and had regular sex with a Frenchman who only learned his "girlfriend's" gender years after the affair. Compared to animals like walruses and elk, which show dramatic physical differences between the sexes, the human body is more androgynous. In courtship we mark ourselves with gender cues to proclaim, as clearly as possible, that we are male or female.

Advertising with stripes, bands, and geometric shapes is a time-tested means of establishing sexuality in the animal world. In the sea bass, a banded, vertically striped body signifies "I am male," while a dark shape on the tail means "I am female." Male guppies and house finches show redder colors than females, and members of both species respond to a male's red coloration in courtship as a gender cue. In human animals of the Western world, a vertically descending necktie suggests "I am male," and a curvilinear drape of fabric on the hips signifies "I am female."

In biology, male and female differences in coloration, markings, size, and behavior are known as *sexual dimorphism*. Some animals, including dogs and cats, show few differences, and we cannot easily identify their sex. Other animals, including lions, peacocks, and mountain gorillas, are obviously male or female, even from afar. A 450-pound silverback male can weigh twice what a female gorilla weighs. As for our species, we are modestly dimorphic from head to toe, with many slight and a few dramatic sexual differences to display. From the shape of our forehead, rounder in women, to the diameter of our toes, thicker in men, we announce our sexual identity and trust the message rings true.

In courtship, the best strategy is to accentuate your body's natural gender signs convincingly to show who you are. This means dramatizing the visible shapes encoded in masculine shoulders and feminine waists as well as enhancing subtle cues like the fullness, height, and shape of your eyebrows. In the Attention Phase, what separates the paired from the unpaired often boils down to geometric details of line, shape, and shadow.

What Eyebrows Divulge

Let's focus for a moment on eyebrows—the two arches of short hairs above our eyes—as a revealing case in point. Note that a woman's eyebrows ride significantly higher over her eyes than a man's do. Male brows hug the top of the bony *eye orbits*, ridges of bone surrounding the eye sockets, which are squarer in men and rounder in women, and closely follow the bone ridges' contours. Female eyebrows—and you can run your fingertip over them to feel the difference—start out on the same bony ridge close to the nose. Then they flare up, lift off the ridge, and arc backward toward the ears. A man's brows lay heavily and horizontally across his nose like a "T." A woman's rise upward in a curvilinear flare above the bridge of her nose like an "S."

These differences make a man's eyes look more deeply set than a woman's. In courtship, this gives him a serious, authoritative, even a stern look. Since her eyebrows frame larger areas of skin beneath their contours—expanses of skin above the eyelids called *supraorbital margins*—a woman's brow line makes her eyes appear more shallowly set and bigger against their background patches of flesh. Eyebrows say more than just "I am male" or "I am female." The uplifted appearance of a woman's eyebrows defines a mood of eagerness, happiness, and "wide-eyed innocence." Masculine brows suggest strength in reserve, whereas feminine designs invite approach with their suggestion of friendliness. A woman's eyebrows signify "I'm harmless"; a man's say "Don't tread on me!"

> The uplifted appearance of a woman's eyebrows defines a mood of eagerness, happiness, and "wide-eyed innocence." Masculine brows suggest strength in reserve, whereas feminine designs invite approach with their suggestion of friendliness.

Straight-across eyebrows bespeak masculinity. Femininity shows in arched brows. Since they announce so boldly, men need only trim their coarse, low-lying brows to convey a male message in courtship. Trimming is recommended because it sends a high-status message: "I am well-groomed." On the female side, since her thinner eyebrows are more subtly expressive than a man's, a woman may do a great deal to enhance their appeal.

A well-placed arch above a woman's iris mimics the friendly appeal of the eyebrow flash of recognition.

The language of eyebrows is arcane. It requires translation by makeup gurus like the late Kevyn Aucoin, and by shaping artist Anastasia, a Beverly Hills consultant to the stars. Anastasia's message is that, though women's eyebrow fashions change, defining a visible arch above the outer corner of each eye remains the same. A well-placed arch above the lateral edge of a woman's iris mimics the friendly appeal of the eyebrow flash of recognition. A talented stylist can transform ordinary eyebrows into beguiling brows in moments. The secret is knowing precisely where and how to place the arch.

CLASSIC COSMETOLOGY: MARILYN'S EYEBROW PEAKS

Few women pay much as attention to their gender cues as Marilyn Monroe did to hers in the 1950s. She was a perfectionist in the design features of her body, especially her eyebrows. Looking at studio photos, we are powerfully drawn to Marilyn's eyes. Nonverbally, she invites us to gaze because her brows lift in defined "peaks" that greet us with a universal sign, the eyebrow flash of recognition. Around the world, the eyebrow flash invites friendly contact with those who see and respond to its call.

A close look at Marilyn's eyebrows reveals that they are not raised at all. Her forehead's *frontalis* muscles, which lift her brows, are completely relaxed. There are no horizontal lines in her forehead to suggest even the slightest muscular contraction. Marilyn Monroe's artfully uplifted eyebrows draw us, because they were designed to seduce by the legendary Hollywood makeup man Whitey Snyder.

Supraorbital margins are bigger in women than in men, but Marilyn's are huge. The radiant skin around her big eyes makes them seem bigger still. In effect, our brain responds to the fleshy

CONTINUED ON NEXT PAGE

area marked by Whitey's lines as to a larger-than-normal eye. The elliptical frames he drew on Marilyn's face bring eyes to hers like the rings of a target bring eyes to a bull's-eye.

Snyder's achievement was in the arches he defined at the midpoints of Marilyn's brows. The angular, pyramidal peaks convince visual centers of the brain that her eyebrows are emotionally "lifting" to invite attention. Whitey penciled peaks in Marilyn's eyebrows precisely above the pupils. "I'd bring them to a peak just outside the center of her eyes," Whitey explained. "You couldn't go out much farther than that or it would look phoney" (Crown, 1987:118). Through Whitey's expertise, Marilyn's eyebrows define an attitude millions still recognize at a glance.

Reveal a Narrow Waist

Geometrically, what is the most attractive female shape in courtship? Some say shapely legs, while others guess shoulders, bosom, hips, or ankles, but they are wrong. Scientific studies confirm that, despite the acknowledged charm of breasts, bottoms, and thighs, the most noticed feature of a woman's body, apart from the face itself, is her waist. Research by anthropologists and evolutionary psychologists finds that the active ingredient of a woman's figure is the visible pinch in her waistline, the "hourglass."

Despite fashion trends and competing cultural norms about what makes a woman's body beautiful—bust size, body weight, hip girth, the circumference of calf muscles—one thing stands clear. Men everywhere consider a thin waist more attractive than a thick one. From Neolithic figurines to classical Egyptian sculptures, from Miss Universe contests to *Playboy,* the message is the same. A constricted waist is prettier than one that bulges.

Men do not judge a fashion model's super-thin waist as significantly more attractive than the waist of a normal-weight female.

How thin is a pretty waist? Studies show that men do not judge a fashion model's super-thin waist as being significantly more attractive than the waist of a normal-weight female. Research by neuropsychologist Devendra Singh found that men do not equate abnormally thin figures with beauty. What attracts is not absolute thinness but the contrast between waist and hips. Anthropologists have found that a low waist-to-hip ratio (computed by dividing waist girth by hip girth) signals fertility and good health—and reassures that the object of a man's affection is not pregnant with another man's child.

In courtship, women with low (less than 1.0) waist-to-hip ratios (centerfolds average 0.67) can accentuate slimness with a belt, waistband, or sash. Women with waists smaller than 1.0, like Nicole Kidman, Jennifer Lopez, and Madonna, look good in light-colored, form-fitting tops worn above dark skirts. The marked contrast brings eyes to the narrow waist. Women with higher ratios—1.0 or above—like Rosie O'Donnell or Queen Latifah, can wear tops with strategically placed patterns and details that draw eyes upward, away from a waist that may suggest "I am pregnant." In response to a message about fertility that was encoded millions of years ago, men still find the sight of a curvaceous waist sexy today.

Wield a Wedge

What is a man's most attractive shape in courtship? Some say muscular arms, while others claim hands, chest, back, or abs. They, too, are wrong. Science has determined that—apart from face and eyes—the most noticed feature of the male body is its essential "wedge" shape. Women prefer men with broad shoulders because an ample torso connotes masculine strength. In controlled studies, men and women judged greater width in a man's shoulders—greater breadth in relation to hip size—more attractive than narrow shoulders. Their size and angularity when squared betoken dominance in the competitive male arena.

Science has determined that—apart from face and eyes—the most noticed feature of the male body is its essential "wedge" shape.

How wide should a man's shoulders be? Women don't insist on the same high standards for men that men exact from women. Women are more forgiving in courtship. While an hourglass shape is essential to attract the male eye—which, as Singh notes, goes to the waist before seeing a face—feminine eyes find smaller masculine shoulders okay if visibly broader than her own. A modest size difference is enough to send the needed message: "male protectiveness." The stronger message encoded in a body-builder's shoulders target other men's eyes as they battle for female attention. The basic wedge shape of a normal-size man is as appealing in courtship as the super-normal frame of a Schwarzenegger.

Before admitting that all masculine shoulder displays are created equal, we should ask why so many males dress in power uniforms for business, politics, and military affairs. The answer is that tailored jackets accent the natural wedge shape. Dressed in T-shirts, Hulk Hogan and Woody Allen appear as members of different species. Wearing padded shoulders, barrel sleeves, flaring lapels, and the dropped hemline of his signature tweed jacket, Woody's attire is suitably "pumped-up" to attract a mate.

Showing Harmlessness—"I Mean No Harm"

In our curious brand of courtship, being present and obviously male or female is not enough. Before approaching an unfamiliar man or woman, you need to know the visible signs to determine if the partner will appreciate your approach. You need reassurance that your prospective mate will not be surly, rude, or unkind. You need, in other words, readable signs of *harmlessness*. Harmlessness is a basic theme in courtship as it is later in marriage itself. In the Western world, a wedding ring on the left hand is a symbol of submission.

Showing harmlessness is an important theme in the courtship of animals. The green heron's *stretch* display, for example, is designed to lure his mate closer by showing he will not attack. Simultaneously stretching his head and neck upward, out of attack position, swaying submissively side to side, and emitting the soft *aaroo-aaroo* call nullifies hostility (Bastock, 1967). The bird also makes bowing movements in the display. Females respond to the male's humble body language by approaching his nest.

Tilting the head sideward says,
"I am interested."

A man may telegraph his unspoken interest through "pigeon toes."

Vulnerable cues give permission to others to come physically near.

In courtship, signs of humility, shyness, and harmlessness are essential. Vulnerable cues give permission to others to come physically near. This is why Monkeyshines women find it easy to approach the imposing football player seated by himself at the far table. Notice the cast on his foot and the thin cane dangling from his chair. His "I am harmless" signals show he is accessible and not likely to bite. Women approach without fear. Visible limps, casts, bandages, eyeglasses, and other signs of weakness elicit a distinctively human *caring response.*

Bare Your Throat

A good way to show harmlessness in the Attention Phase is to undo the top button of your shirt or blouse and bare the throat. This shows the "neck dimple," the fleshy hollow at the front of your neck below the Adam's apple and above the collarbone. Unclothed, the anatomical indent reveals itself through our upright posture and hairless skin. To mask the frailty in business, government, and military affairs, we hide the dimple behind a knotted tie, scarf, or turtleneck for a show of formality and strength. A bundled neck says, "Keep your distance." In courtship, the neck dimple makes a submissive appeal for all to see. Its fragility says, "You may approach."

Showing the throat says, "I am harmless—you may approach."

Submissive throat-baring has been studied in dogs, wolves, fish, and reptiles. Crocodiles lift their heads out of water to show the throat when dominant males swim by, or else face a fight. Baring the neck prevents attack with an unspoken message of harmlessness: "I give up." So appealing is the neck dimple in courtship, as we face each other across a room, table, or dance floor, that culturally diverse fashion statements have evolved to exhibit and adorn the throat. Low-neckline dresses, peasant blouses, and classic V-neck tops are popular around the world.

So appealing is the neck dimple in courtship, as we face each other across a room, table, or dance floor, that culturally diverse fashion statements have evolved to exhibit and adorn the throat.

For women, a short strand of pearls or a gold-beaded chain brings eyes to the disarming recess by marking the skin beneath it with a line.

With its eye-catching splash of color, an amber, turquoise, or coral pendant worn beneath the clavicle brings attention to the dimple as well. Properly placed below for accent, a quarter-size pendant makes a submissive statement. It marks but does not cover the concavity as a formal choker would.

In traditional societies, shirtless men commonly wear necklaces, while men in the West wear buttoned shirts and ties. The best way for Western males to show the disarming neck dimple is to remove or loosen their ties and undo their shirt buttons at the throat. This lowers the power coefficient, making it easier for women to draw near. Showing the neck's vulnerable, crepey flesh adds an easygoing informality, even as the shirt-collar's sides rise to enhance the masculinity of a man's thicker neck: "I am male; I mean no harm."

Move Your Shoulders

Another sign of friendly intention is the shrug display. Take note when one or both of your partner's shoulders lift toward the ears or flex forward in front. Since the motions are fleeting, you need to watch carefully to read their cues. Shoulders elevate as *trapezius* and *levator scapulae* muscles raise the shoulder blades. Shoulders bend when trapezius muscles (assisted by *pectoralis major, minor,* and *serratus anterior*) ventrally flex the shoulders forward. There are no better signs to show how a partner feels about being approached.

The shoulder shrug is a sign of yielding. Submissively lifted shoulders invite a partner closer. Seeing the cue reveals one is unlikely to step back, turn away, or brush off the advance. We unconsciously flex and lift our shoulders with those we like. It's called the *cute response.* Our shoulders move the same way when we cuddle babies to show we care.

A lifted shoulder says,
"I am interested."

We unconsciously flex and lift our shoulders with those we like. It's called the *cute response*. Our shoulders move the same way when we cuddle babies to show we care.

FIELD NOTES: SUCCESSFUL IN SEATTLE

At Monkeyshines, Leather Vest's hyperactive hand gestures and roving eyes attracted too much attention; they kept women away. Now let's observe the quiet poise of a nearby rival—who also sits alone at an empty table—as his composed demeanor brings women near. In the Attention Phase, courtship, like Zen, is paradoxically indirect. The less actively you strive, the more quickly you reach your goal.

"Denim Jacket," with a toothpick in his mouth, is reading the *Wall Street Journal*. His reading is intense. He holds the paper in both hands, close to his face, and his eyes visibly move across the page. The jean jacket and the *Journal* make an eye-catching juxtaposition. Since he is so absorbed in his reading, a woman could easily slide in beside him without saying a word. No greeting, no head-nod, no eye-contact required. Denim is so wrapped up he seems easier to approach than his rival, Leather Vest, who moves

CONTINUED ON NEXT PAGE

his eyes too eagerly in anticipation. Because of his low profile, Denim lures a woman into his territory within minutes of occupying it. After preparatory head tosses, head bows, palm shows, and a deferential shrug of his shoulders, a conversation begins.

If you cannot achieve love at first sight, you can achieve attention at first sight.

The first stage of courtship is for attracting attention. Phase One is the time to let people know you are present, male or female, and approachable. You go through the Attention Phase before speaking or touching. The stages unfold in a serial order laid down eons ago in the evolution of vertebrates. Phase One is not the time to pursue. It is the time to let yourself be seen.

3. PHASE TWO: HOW TO READ THE GLEAM IN AN EYE

The males of many species display to females immediately
before mating: they dance, posture, call, and otherwise
behave peculiarly and conspicuously.
—MARGARET BASTOCK

COURTSHIP'S PHASE ONE is a bid for attention, a time to send messages about physical presence, gender, and "safeness" for all to see. Now, in Phase Two, the Recognition Phase, you read unspoken reactions to diagnose how a partner feels: Does she notice? Is he interested? How do I know?

The Recognition Phase is mainly nonverbal. Though you may speak, you do not yet express feelings in words. It is simply too soon and too risky to confide in a stranger. By opening up, you face rejection. Since the emotional pain of rejection is like the physical pain of a punch to the stomach—neurologically, both register in the *anterior cingulate cortex* of the forebrain—you naturally hold back.

In the second stage of courtship, you proceed with caution to avoid getting hurt. Before laying yourself open, you decipher gestures and demeanor to gauge a partner's willingness to be near you and to assess the likelihood of a kind response. The underlying communication is like a bat's sonar: you bounce Attention Phase cues off people and read the gestural echoes.

The first rule of body language, established in the 1970s by anthropologist Ray Birdwhistell, is that a person cannot *not* behave.

Should a partner try to show "absolutely nothing," the immobility itself would speak. Indeed, a stilled body tells its tale just as a moving body does. People make significantly fewer hand gestures while deceiving, for example, than while telling the truth. Motionless hands, studies confirm, can signal deceit.

> The first rule of body language is that a person cannot *not* behave.

Whether you move your hands in courtship or keep them as still as a statue's, the signals themselves are, for the most part, out of your conscious control. Moreover, reading body-language cues is largely unconscious as well. The pupils of your eyes are a good illustration. We know that pupils constrict and dilate in response to light and darkness, but they also expand and contract in response to emotions, feelings, and moods.

Research with a measuring device called a *pupillometer* reveals that a man's pupils enlarge when he looks at photos of an attractive woman. Nerves in his spinal cord's *superior cervical ganglion* activate dilator muscles to widen the aperture of his iris. In turn, a woman's pupils dilate when she notices a well-proportioned man in a swimsuit but constrict when she sees him au naturel, without his trunks. In these circumstances, pupil dilation correlates with "liking" and constriction with "disliking." An unclothed male body is not as attractive to women as the female form is to men.

Though you may think pupil size is too tiny to be noticed, psychologists have learned that we do see—and measurably respond to—a partner's constricted or dilated eyes. In a classic study, men who were shown nearly identical photographs of a pretty woman consistently picked the photo with artificially enlarged pupils as more attractive, though they couldn't say why (Hess, 1975).

That she seemed prettier was because her dilated eyes emitted a recognition cue the men quite unconsciously decoded as a positive sign. Bigger pupils seemed to say "I like you." This is why, centuries ago, European women dilated their pupils with a cosmetic extract of belladonna. *Belladonna*, which means "beautiful lady" in Italian, helped them beckon with attractive eyes. Today, savvy poker players read pupil dilation as a "tell," meaning the opponent holds an attractive hand.

> It is hard to spot pupil dilation, especially if the person has dark eyes. But my experience with hypnosis has helped me identify cues related to this phenomenon. When I hypnotize someone, I read pupils as well as eyes. I observe that when a person dilates the pupils, the gaze appears to stare, empty and vacant. So, when I see these expressions in a person's gaze, even if he or she is far away, I know the pupils are dilated.
>
> —Marco Pacori, psychologist

Most recognition cues are easier to read than pupil size, though with practice, a person can accurately decipher pupils at distances up to six feet. When correctly decoded, a Phase Two signal reveals how interested or available someone may be. A man should remember that in the early stages of courtship women are better observers than men. In fact, women are more sensitive to nonverbal signals from childhood on, which helps explain "women's intuition." Yet neither women nor men can usually list—sign for sign—the specific signals that led them to know when someone seemed interested or seemed not to care.

To make the Recognition Phase more explicit on a conscious level, I will break down and analyze its nonverbal cues. Since no recognition cue is foolproof, you should base your appraisal on as many signs as possible. A single promising sign does not a courtship make. Courtship is intrinsically ambivalent. It is natural for partners to feel like approaching and avoiding you at the same time. Mixed messages in human courtship are as common as they are in the courtship of mammals and birds.

A MISMATCHED COURTSHIP: MAN AND BIRD

In one of biology's stranger experiments, a human being successfully courted a whooping crane (Walters, 1988). Between 1976 and 1982, ornithologist George Archibald courted a five-foot tall female crane named "Tex." Shortly after hatching, Tex was mistakenly sexed as a male and given a masculine name.

The unlikely pairing took place in a captive breeding program at the International Crane Foundation in Baraboo, Wisconsin. On the foundation's grounds, George sent Tex all the right attention-getting signals. He faced her directly, flapped his arms, and bobbed his head up and down. Tex returned George's mimicked crane signals with recognition cues of her own. She squared her body with his, flapped her wings, bobbed her head, and "danced." Clearly, the bird recognized George as a mate.

As the curious courtship progressed, George and Tex danced together in syncopated rhythm: As George bowed, Tex rose, and as Tex bowed, George rose, and so on, in alternation, to establish the essential synchrony needed for mating. Whenever George lost his rhythm, the female seemed to lose interest in the courtship. But when he got it right, Tex would tempt him further still. She would spread her wings widely, turn her back to him, and push up on her tiptoes into the typical mating posture of a female crane. Her seductive pose was an enticement for George to have sex.

Precisely at this point in their courtship, George's fellow biologists intervened and artificially inseminated the love-struck bird. George Archibald's experiment had been designed to arouse the hormonal ardor required for Tex to ovulate. Since she was raised in captivity by humans, Tex never learned how to relate properly to cranes, nor could she produce an egg. So Archibald became Tex's faithful companion for the sake of begetting another member of her endangered species.

This courtship, like many between men and human females, took several years to produce an offspring. On June 1, 1982, Tex's artificially inseminated egg hatched, and tiny "Gee Whiz" was born. By sending the right Attention and Recognition Phase signals, the mismatched couple danced together, saw eye-to-eye, and bridged the species gap.

POSITIVE RECOGNITION CUES

In courtship's Attention Phase you send messages about presence: "I am here." In the Recognition Phase you watch for messages of response. Your partner may be interested when you see:

- *Rapid eyeblinks.* Faster blink rates reflect emotional excitement, as the excitatory neurochemical dopamine is released into the brain.
- The *chameleon effect.* Imitating your body movements shows when a partner is truly on your wavelength.
- *Blushing.* From slight reddening at the top of the ears to a full facial flush, a reddish hue reveals when your partner's sympathetic nervous system has engaged.
- *Hair preening.* Seeing another's self-preening gestures as you approach means "I'm interested."
- An *intention cue.* An arm casually extended in your direction across a tabletop signals a wish to touch.
- *Forward lean.* Prompted by the *orienting reflex,* people lean toward whatever—or whomever—they find most important at the time.
- *Wide eyes.* When your partner's central nervous system is aroused, involuntary visceral muscles of the eyelids produce rounder-than-normal eyes.
- A *jaw droop.* When you capture full attention, your partner's lips visibly part. A jaw droop is your cue to move closer.
- *Gaze crossing.* A partner's alternating gaze, back and forth across your field of view, signals the desire to establish eye contact.

In the Blink of an Eye

You see a sign of approval when the person sitting across a table establishes eye contact, blinks rapidly, and gazes away. A *rapid eyeblink* (or "eyelash flutter") means you've raised the blinker's level of psychological arousal. Faster-than-normal eye-closing and -opening movements show you've registered on the partner's radar screen.

Blink rate reflects arousal in the manner of a polygraph test. The normal resting rate of a human is twenty closures per minute, with the average blink lasting one quarter of a second (Karson, 1992). Significantly faster rates reflect emotional excitement and stress, like that aroused in the fight-or-flight response. A study by Boston College psychologist Joseph Tecce found that, under intense pressure in the 1996 U.S. presidential debates, candidate Bob Dole averaged 147 blinks a minute—seven times the normal rate of twenty. President Bill Clinton, meanwhile, averaged ninety-nine blinks a minute, reaching 117 when asked about increases in teen drug use, a sensitive issue of the day.

Both sexes blink faster with partners they like.

In courtship, faster blinking may reflect sexual excitement. Batting the eyelashes is a familiar flirting cue seen around the world. Wearing mascara or artificial lashes embellishes the blink. By disclosing her excitement, a woman telegraphs that she feels attracted. Eye batting is not just a feminine cue. Studies show that both sexes blink faster with partners they like.

How do you read someone's blinking rate without a stopwatch? Simply monitor the partner's resting rate as he or she gazes elsewhere, then compare the rate with what you see in eye contact. You needn't count the blinks, only judge which is faster.

Stirred-up feelings stimulate the brain stem's *reticular activating system* (RAS), a primitive arousal center over which we have little control. The RAS acts on the midbrain to release the excitatory chemical dopamine into reptilian vision centers (the superior colliculi). These unthinking, unconscious centers control the blink reflex. Like pupil size, rapid eyeblink is entirely out of awareness, making it a trustworthy recognition cue.

The Sincerest Form of Flattery

Having established from pupils and eyelids when a stranger across a table is interested, the next sign to watch for is "same behavior" or *isopraxism*. Does the person imitate, copy, or mimic your action: cross legs when you cross, lean back when you lean back, or hair-preen as you preen? If so, assume there is more than superficial interest in your presence. Studies by anthropologists, psychologists, and psychiatrists agree that isopraxism—also known as mimicry, synchrony, paralleling, mirroring, postural echo, and the chameleon effect—reveals when two people like each other.

Fondness shows when you act alike, move in unison, and use the same gestures, postures, and vocal tones. Isopraxism is a natural form of animal rapport found in the courtship of reptiles, mammals, and birds. Before mating, great crested grebes (waterbirds known for their graceful courtship ballet) rise up breast-to-breast and sway together in what biologists call a *penguin dance*. Red-crested cranes stretch their necks and vertically point their bills in tandem to reinforce courting vows with a *unison call*. In humans, close friends sit together at a table, lean their chins on fisted hands, and chat like reflected images. In a crowded bar, should you adopt the chin-on-fist posture—and see it mimicked from a neighboring table by someone glancing your way— the mirrored gesture may signal attraction.

Mirroring takes place with or without eye contact. Frequently, the stranger will seem to gaze past you, or off to one side, before synching into a clear postural echo. This happens as the wish to approach, signaled by the echo, competes with an equal but opposite wish to avoid, signaled by averted gaze. In the Recognition Phase, ambivalent signals are commonly exchanged before partners speak. They result from what biologists call *motivational conflict*. Motivational conflict is found in the courtship of human beings as well as in that of monkeys, butterflies, bowerbirds, and many other animals. Before speaking with someone new, "should I or shouldn't I?" is a common refrain.

To test a partner's isopraxism, shift from your chin-on-fist posture to another position. Pull away from the table and lean back in your chair. If the person follows suit—and there may be a five- or ten-second delay in the echoed shift—you have reason to believe the mirroring is not a chance occurrence but rather a positive recognition cue.

A cting alike is psychologically reassuring to the animal mind.

In much the same way, a female Canada goose recognizes her mate by returning the movements he presents to her (Ogilvie, 1978). She flatters him with imitation, because, in courtship, acting alike is psychologically reassuring. To the animal mind, sameness equates with safety. Same is safe, emotionally—and safe is same.

Courting birds, like smitten humans, mimic each other to draw closer in space.

Isopraxism Is Courtship's Glue

Isopraxism, the scientific name for our imitative response, was coined by neuroanatomist Paul MacLean in 1975. In Greek *iso* is "same" and *praxis* is "behavior." Isopraxism is based on a deep, reptilian principle of mimicry that leads us to copy, emulate, and repeat the actions of those we find attractive. MacLean located the imitation response in a primitive motor center of our forebrain called the *basal ganglia.*

Isopraxism explains why we dress like our colleagues and adopt the beliefs, mannerisms, and even the voice tones of people we admire. Wearing the same team jersey or franchise cap to look alike suggests that we think and feel alike as well.

A growing body of research shows that mimicking the postures, actions, and clothing of others facilitates interaction and increases liking (Chartrand and Bargh, 1999). It seems we can't help but like those who are just like us. Psychologist Albert Mehrabian observed that when people imitate each other's mannerisms and voice tones to be more alike, they communicate an implicit desire to approach.

In animals, isopraxism shows in the simultaneous head-nodding of lizards, in the group gobbling of turkeys, and in the synchronous preening of birds. In the courtship of mallard ducks, mates relate through isopraxism as they head-bob in syncopated rhythm, preen-behind-wing together, and dip their bills in unison to drink from a pond. In human courtship, couples head nod in tandem as they speak, preen their tresses in synchrony, and sip champagne in unison as they toast.

Isopraxism reveals how unacquainted couples feel as well. Sitting near each other at a party, unpaired men and women may unthinkingly lift their glasses in silent synchrony and sip together as if they were already paired. You can see who likes whom by noting who imitates whom. Copying another's posture, stance, or mannerisms makes you seem more alike and subliminally more "likable." In courtship's second stage, doing the same thing paves the way for more romantic same-doings in the future.

Mimicking another person's posture says, "I'm just like you. I'm safe. Trust me."

The Color of Interest

Like our animal kin we, too, change color in courtship. A chimpanzee's bottom turns pink to show her receptiveness to mates. A seahorse blushes orange as he courts his mate. The face of a smitten man or woman blushes red.

In the Recognition Phase, one may redden in response to a partner's physical closeness. All of a sudden one's forehead, cheeks, neck, and even the upper chest glow in embarrassed, awkward shyness. A symptom of stranger anxiety, blushing takes place as the sympathetic nervous system dilates small blood vessels in the face and body. "In most cases," Charles Darwin observed more than a century ago, "the face, ears and neck are the sole parts which redden; but many persons, whilst blushing intensely, feel that their whole bodies grow hot and tingle . . ." (Darwin, 1872:312).

Helen, a twenty-five-year-old college student, has a personal sense of the blush. "I have noticed in my own experience that blushing in a man is a pretty reliable indicator that he finds me physically alluring." Not everyone blushes the same way, and some do not blush at all. In Phase Two, a person without an obviously flushed face may show slight reddening atop the ears. A beginning or partial blush, revealed in reddish hues on the ear flap's rounded upper helix, is often the first visible sign that a man or woman feels more than a neighborly mood coming on. In many parts of the world, women apply crimson pigments to their cheeks to mimic the rosy glow of sexual attraction signaled by the blush.

Some people blush uncontrollably in almost any social setting. An estimated 10 to 15 percent of all human beings have some degree of *social anxiety disorder* and turn red with every stranger they meet. In courtship, a "super-blusher" may give off false-positive signals. A few suffer enough to elect a surgical procedure known as *thorascopic sympathecotomy.* Sympathetic nerves to the face are severed, and blushing is no longer possible, even in courtship.

A Summoning Hair Preen

Another positive cue is the *hair preen.* Both men and women touch, hold, and run fingers through their hair in the company of people they find attractive. Hair preens bring attention to the face through motions of the hand and fingers themselves, and through movements of the tresses, curls, and bangs. Psychiatrist Albert Scheflen classified preening as a come-hither signal. Handling, twirling, fluffing, and combing the hair, Scheflen observed, are unconscious ways to say "I am interested. I like you. Notice me" (Fast, 1970:108).

> Can you tell me what is going on when a man sitting at a conference table leans in the direction of a woman sitting at the same table and absently strokes his own hair? I seem to get this a lot at work, and it's really puzzling to me. I keep thinking it's related to apes and grooming—or possibly to some little-kid thing.
>
> —Linda

Like a flushed face, spontaneous hair preening shows emotions stirred by the sympathetic nervous system. We preen when emotions run high to release pent-up feelings brought on by a nice-looking partner's allure. The principle is not unlike that of acupressure massage. Fondling our hair follicles stimulates tactile nerve endings in the scalp and refocuses attention inward, away from the stranger "out there" who has us on pins and needles.

Preening is common in the courtship of mammals and birds. Animals show willingness to mate by conspicuously cleaning their feathers or fur to show "contact readiness." In its preening display, the mallard duck draws his bill along the underside of his partly lifted wing to make a loud *rrr* sound. He reveals an attractive, blue-feather patch exposed by the raised wing (Bastock, 1967). In humans, preening brings attention to the luster, sheen, and style of attractively groomed hair. When the hair preen you give is returned by another, you're clearly on the same page.

Your Intentions Are Showing

Motives are clear in the telling signs biologists call *intention movements*. Many courting displays originate from incomplete, preparatory gestures that signal something is about to happen. When a dog's lips lift to show teeth as you reach for his bone, you witness an *intention display*. Rather than bite you, Fido shows the beginning phase of the biting sequence to bluff you away. When a cat arches her back before attacking or fleeing from a neighboring feline, the conspicuous hump is an intention signal as well. The threatened cat's spine bows upward as her retreating front end backs up against her advancing rear. The ambivalent posture shows an intention to back away and to attack at the same time.

In courtship, the transparency of intention cues can make people reading an easy matter. When a man finds a woman attractive, instead of telling her in words, he may extend an arm partway across a table, as if preparing to touch her forearm or hand. As with other intention signs, the preparatory action will not actually be completed. He will stop short of making physical contact, but his desire to touch is clearly signaled by the reach. An arm advanced in her direction is, without forethought or plan, a message of interest.

A telling intention cue is the *knees clasp*. From a seated position, leaning forward and clasping both knees with the hands means "I am about to leave" (Morris, 1994:149). Should a woman clasp her knees when a man walks by, she telegraphs an intention to follow him but without actually following through. She may sit in the upright-and-locked "ready" position several moments before leaving her chair. The knees clasp suggests that, in her own mind, she has already left.

Which Way Are You Leaning?

When a man leans toward a woman seated nearby, his posture suggests he'd like to move nearer. The stranger barrier keeps him from actually scooting his chair closer, but the wish to advance clearly shows in the lean. Like pupil size, *forward lean* is a sign most read unconsciously. You sense that the person bent in your direction—who is, after all, just sitting there sipping a latte—seems primed to approach. Psychologists classify forward leaning as a friendly or "immediate" cue. Before speaking, couples may lean in as if teetering on the brink of conversation. Aiming at each other says, "We need to get closer."

Forward lean is a mood sign controlled by the *orienting reflex* (OR). The OR is a primitive response that alerts us to whatever—or whomever—we find most important in our sensory surroundings at the time. We needn't think about it since the OR decides. Drawn to a special someone across a room, the OR automatically contracts muscles of the body wall to tilt the spinal column toward he or she who fanned desire.

Forward lean is a mood sign controlled by the *orienting re-flex* (OR). The OR is a primitive response that alerts us to whatever—or whomever—we find most important in our sensory surroundings at the time.

Bending motions of the trunk or *axial* body are more fundamental as mood signs than movements of the arms and legs. Axial muscles are older. Unlike limb muscles of the *appendicular* body, which are specialized for walking, climbing, and reaching, trunk muscles are generalized. They are less subject to deliberate control. Early in our evolution as vertebrates, millions of years before limbs evolved, simple body-bending movements advanced us toward mates and away from enemies.

Anatomically, dividing the skeleton into primary trunk and secondary limbs is based on function rather than mere form or convention (Horne, 1995). Our most basic body language comes not from motions of the limbs but from primal actions of the body wall. In the Recognition Phase, watch the trunk for telling "locomotion" movements. Does your partner's upper body angle toward you or twist away? Forward or backward bending motions of the torso—as people approach or avoid you—reveal where they truly stand.

Forward or backward bending motions of the torso—as people approach or avoid you—reveal where they truly stand.

Big Eyes Like What They See

Wide eyes is another recognition cue. It shows when a stranger meets your gaze with wider-than-normal eyes. Maximally opening the upper and lower eyelids, sometimes called "flashbulb eyes," happens when one feels strong physical attraction. In anatomical terms, the *palpebral fissures* dilate to show greater whiteness, roundness, and protrusion of the eyeballs.

Children make "big eyes," the wide-eyed look of innocence you see as they excitedly greet your approach. In the Recognition Phase, big eyes show that your partner's stranger anxiety has been displaced by eagerness to advance. Two involuntary, visceral eyelid muscles, the *superior* and *inferior tarsals*, dilate the eye slits to reflect the emotional excitement.

A visceral sign, wide eyes is hard to conceal and difficult to produce at will. Though you may consciously open your eyes wider, maximal dilation depends on contraction of the tarsals. Controlled by sympathetic nerves through the *superior cervical ganglia*, these impulsive muscles in the upper and lower eyelids make wide eyes an accurate barometer of mood.

Reading a Droopy Jaw

Wide eyes may be accompanied by a parted-lips expression called the *jaw droop*. In 1872, Charles Darwin included "opening of the mouth" along with wide eyes as a sign of attention and surprise. Darwin attributed the drooping jaw to muscle relaxation, claiming that amazement "absorbs" bodily energy. In a crowded elevator, we keep our jaws nearly closed and our lips sealed. Background muscle tone in the *masseter, temporalis,* and *medial pterygoid* muscles contributes to the "blank face" we show in public places.

Our reserved, blank-face expression keeps strangers away. But should an attractive stranger catch our eyes, the background brainstem impulses controlling the lower jaw's resting muscle tone are temporarily blocked. Strongly aroused emotion causes our mandible to drop of its own weight. We lose control for the moment, and it shows in our lips as they part.

Dramatic jaw droops are staples of science-fiction thrillers as signs of horror given while confronting colossal apes, giant lizards, and alien spacecraft. Overcome by emotion, we lose muscle tone in the lower jaw. In courtship, less melodramatic jaw droops reflect desire brought on by sexual attraction. Parted lips are familiar in love scenes as couples bring their faces into alignment for the first kiss. A jaw droop given as eyes meet across a room says, "I'm overcome by you."

Crossing Lines of Sight

In the *gaze cross*, a stranger shows readiness to establish eye contact without looking at you first. Being the first to look has its dangers. You might not return the favor. Not looking back would put the stranger in an uncomfortable position, that of being rebuffed. Since unilateral gaze may backfire, he or she saves face and instead gazes across your field of view to test the waters by signaling an intention to gaze. When your eyes finally do meet, it's hard to know who looked first.

The typical gaze cross unfolds like this. A woman looks up from her newspaper and glances to her left, toward something indefinite, then sweeps her eyes right, across a man's field of view toward something equally remote, and finally brings her eyes back to the paper. In the gaze cross, she repeatedly crisscrosses her line of sight back and forth across his. The woman doesn't rest her eyes on his, but she need not; her back-and-forth movements catch his notice and pique his curiosity.

The outcome is predictable. The man reads her body language as an unspoken bid for attention. Her conspicuous head turns proffer an opportunity to gaze off to his left and then to his right, across her field of view. Their lines of vision cross like searchlights in the sky, and forthwith meet head-on in eye contact. Since they correctly read each other's intentions beforehand, the final eye to eye "takes," and their eyes converge without repelling. The couple locks into gaze without either having been first to look.

When You Are Overlooked

The most discouraging sign in courtship is no sign at all. At a party, no reaction—the typical "nonperson" treatment you see in ticket lines, waiting rooms, and elevators—can be as daunting as hostility; at least the latter is a reaction. When you smile, nod, and give the permissible one- or two-second gaze at a party, you expect more than a blank face and disengaged eyes.

> The most discouraging signal in courtship is no signal at all.

No reaction is disheartening because it signals "I'm not interested." In courtship, men and women respond differently when overlooked. A neutral response prompts a woman to seek attention elsewhere. Like water, she wisely flows in the direction of least resistance. A man tends to misread the cue. Less adept at body language, he assumes all is well when a woman barely tolerates his presence. Enchanted by her face and figure, he tunes out her behavior.

This brand of male psychology is known as *Pygmalionism*—falling in love with statues. In Greek mythology, Pygmalion carved and fell in love with a statue. Aphrodite, the goddess of love and beauty, later turned the stoney figure into a real woman, Galatea. In real life, there is the case of a Russian man arrested for paying moonlight visits to the statue of a nymph, and of a Parisian gardener who fell deeply in love with a statue of Venus. Some men pay court whether a woman recognizes them or not. In the process, they neglect those nearby who send come-hither cues. These are the men who have "bad luck" finding dates.

Since it's unfriendly, no reaction can be enough to end a relationship before it begins. Still, initial indifference should not dissuade you from retesting—approaching again—to learn if the someone you notice cares about noticing you. In many cases, unresponsiveness stems from shyness. Studies show that 50 percent of adults in the United States are chronically shy.

NEGATIVE CUES

Courtship is a selective process. In the Recognition Phase, not all signals are positive:

- *No reaction.* When your bid for attention is completely ignored, you receive courtship's most discouraging sign.
- *Freezing.* A stilled body looks like no reaction but signals shyness instead of indifference. The brittle body language of shy people—who constitute 50 percent of the adult population—makes them seem less approachable than they really are.
- *Cold shoulder.* A dismissive turning away to one side means "Do not disturb."
- *Lip squeeze.* Compressed lips suggest that your partner is in no mood to partner with you.

The Big Freeze

Postural immobility or *freezing* resembles no reaction. But shyness, not indifference, is what keeps people perfectly still. A mammalian behavior, motionlessness comes from the death-feigning posture some call *playing possum.* Animals freeze their movements so predators lose interest and call off the attack. In courtship, shy people go rigid near partners they like. A woman clamps her hands tightly in her lap; a man pulls his elbows tightly into his sides. Each remains "paralyzed" like a wax figure until the partner goes away. What looks like disinterest in reality is fear.

S hy people go rigid near partners they like.

Shyness is the most common social phobia. It affects men and women equally. Shyness comes from overactive "flight" tendencies in the fight-or-flight response. Diagnostic clues are gaze aversion, a dry mouth, a low speaking voice, rolled-in lips, lip biting, abnormal sweating, fewer speaking gestures, self-touching, arm-crossing, and holding the upper arms rigidly into the body. These behaviors, some of which are found in other primates, are controlled by the central nucleus of the amygdala.

From the inhibited body language, you might judge a shy person to be unkind. In fact, the opposite is more likely true. Timid people simply care too much about what others think for their own good. They would like to be friendly if only they could unlock their faces and rigid limbs. Friends often say, "When we first met, I thought you didn't like me."

Shy adults are paradoxically drawn to outgoing people, whose animated body language they find highly attractive. Unable to send warm wishes of their own, they fancy those who can. In courtship, you should never assume a frozen face is unapproachable. Instead, do what shyness clinics teach:

1. Physically approach the other person.
2. Make eye contact.
3. Say hello.
4. Maintain a conversation for five minutes.

Demeanor thaws as familiarity engages, and head tilts, palm shows, and head nods emerge.

Courtship's Conundrum: The Cold Shoulder

The *cold shoulder* is a dismissive turning away of the upper body to disregard another person. Given to you, the uncaring shoulder is a clear sign: "Go away."

The cold shoulder is a universal gesture that originates in early childhood from an innate protective response. On instinct, babies turn from strange, looming adults as if they "know" they're in harm's way. They squirm away without ever having had a bad experience with strangers.

On the street, pedestrians turn a cold shoulder to deflect the accosting panhandler: "Stay away." Seeing your partner's shoulder deflect as you sit on a neighboring bar stool means the same. In courtship, it's best to heed the silent warning. Wait until he or she comes out from behind the nonverbal wall before speaking. Better still, sit near someone with warm shoulders.

Tight Lips Deter Friendships

Often hidden in courtship, feelings show clearly in lips. The least amount of tension triggers visible tightening of their intricate musculature. The *lip squeeze* is a usually negative cue exhibited when both lips press together tightly and disappear into a single thin line. Tensed or tightened lips could be a sign that your partner is shy, that you have moved too close too soon, or that you are not appreciated.

The prime mover of *lip compression* is an emotionally sensitive muscle, the *orbicularis oris*. This sphincter muscle runs completely around the mouth opening. On command of the emotional brain, it tightens as if to seal others out. Chimpanzees, gorillas, and orangutans compress their lips in aggression. Tribal New Guinea men press their lips together in anger, just as grumpy singles do in New York. The best strategy in courtship is to defer your opening line until you see relaxed lips.

IN THE RECOGNITION Phase, nonverbal signals tell you to step up or step back. Seeing positive cues beforehand makes it easier to start a conversation. You know your partner is eager to speak before a word is spoken.

4. PHASE THREE: EXCHANGING WORDS

Words lead to deeds.
—UNKNOWN

AFTER DECIPHERING BODY-LANGUAGE cues to gauge a partner's eagerness to be near, you reach courtship's third plateau: the Conversation Phase. Talking to a stranger is a formidable step in the progression toward intimacy. As you will see, some couples become trapped in nonverbal dialogue, as if unable to utter a word. Most do talk and move ahead on courtship's path, beyond posturing, to speech.

To speak, you turn your face toward a partner, who responds by facing you and gazing into your eyes. Conversation momentarily locks you together in an exclusive mini habitat, an "ecological huddle" occupied by the two of you alone. The focus is intense. As a courting duo, you scan each other's eyes, lips, cheeks, and eyebrows for positive cues. Lifted brows, flushed cheeks, parted lips, and a returned gaze are generally favorable signs. According to communication researcher Judee Burgoon, head-nodding, vocal pleasantness, and relaxed laughter "connote greater attraction, liking, trust, affiliation, depth, similarity, and rapport" (Burgoon, 1994:256).

A frequently asked question is: "How long should I look?" Brainwave (*electroencephalogram* or EEG) research and skin conductance (*gal-*

vanic skin resistance or GSR) studies show that gazing too intently in a conversation can lead to discomfort or embarrassment. Direct eye-to-eye contact makes the already close quarters of our personal-casual zone (1.5 to 4 feet in front of the body) feel closer still. In Phase Three, the optimal strategy when speaking to strangers is to alternate your line of sight every three to five seconds between gazing at and gazing away. A shifting gaze pattern, toward and then away, shows interest without seeming too intense.

I have a rather interesting nonverbal situation that has been moving along for almost two years. I met a rather powerful male political figure who, on our first meeting, engaged in heavy eye contact, lip pouts, palm-up displays, open stance, self-touch (back of the head and face)—and, at the end of our first meeting, a quick wink. I encouraged this with an involuntary head tilt, smiles, side glances, and the like. I think it was very unusual for both of us to behave this way. I still have brief visits with him, and I am overpowered by his visual attention. He attempts to engage me in eye contact that lasts longer than a few seconds, and I react by gazing away, squinting, and grimacing. I would like to be more direct, but the situation is very overwhelming. This interaction is disquieting, and I would like to figure out what is going on.

—Kathy

To avert gaze, you can face away by contracting neck muscles that turn your head sideways or keep a steady head and rotate your eyeballs in their sockets. With a new partner the latter option is best. Roll your eyes downward to look away without moving your face. This relieves the strain of staring without suggesting, as a head movement to the right or left might, that your attention has shifted as well. With down-rolled eyes you still "face" the partner.

No Place to Hide

Think of courtship's third stage as an oral exam in which to test your partner's emotional intelligence. As gestures accompany words, they reveal unspoken enthusiasms and attitudes about life and living. Her face flashes feelings of delight or sadness. His body acts out moods in exuberant or muted tones.

The Conversation Phase begins a deep probing. You pose questions and visually monitor replies. Neurologist Richard Restak writes, "Thoughts and emotions are interwoven: every thought, however bland, almost always carries with it some emotional undertone, however subtle" (Restak, 1995:21). Undertones emerge in voice qualities, facial expressions, and gestures. In this prolonged period of face-to-face closeness, your partner's body movements and the emotions for which they stand are plainly open to view. Phase Three is challenging for both of you. The sheer physical proximity in which a conversation takes place gives you no place to hide.

In the Conversation Phase, topics matter less than speaking itself. Biologist Desmond Morris has found that much of what couples say carries little meaning in the semantic sense. "Hey," "What's happening?" and "How are you?" are versions of what Morris calls *grooming talk*. Just as monkeys and apes show affection when they groom a mate's fur, we show friendly intentions with words that mean little more than "I notice you."

Verbal reinforcers—"uh-huh," "that's right," "okay," "sure," "yeah," "all right"—are affiliation signs that demonstrate your eagerness to approach and be approached.

A TONGUE-TIED TWOSOME

Reaching the Conversation Phase is never guaranteed. Consider the case of two single parents, Tom and Megan. Megan came to me for advice about how she might somehow "actually talk" to Tom. Sunday after Sunday, she disclosed, the couple traded attention and recognition cues after church as they visited outside with members of the congregation. Without speaking to each other, they exchanged eye contact, head tilts, smiles, and shy "pigeon toes" cues across a distance of twenty feet. Megan recognized the behaviors as flirtatious and noted that she and Tom often broke eye contact in synchrony by glancing down at their feet. Yet despite clear come-hither signals—exchanged for six months—the couple remained twenty feet apart. Tom and Megan were stranded in what anthropologist Edward Hall has called *the public zone*.

Megan was very interested in Tom. She knew his name because her daughters went to school with his sons. I agreed that Tom's boyish demeanor disclosed an interest in her. Why, then, was this seemingly smitten couple unable to proceed to the Conversation Phase? Why, after six months, were they still unable to speak?

"I can never think what to say," Megan said, "and maybe it's the same for him. We just stand there and then we drive off. I feel really awkward about it and I'm sure he does, too."

What Megan, Tom, and other speechless couples need to know is that words themselves count more than topics. Whatever Megan might say to Tom, it need not be witty, charming, or clever. Tom would perceive the simple act of her saying something—anything at all—as a friendly gesture inviting him to talk back. Just saying "Hello" would suffice. In courtship, the first words are little more than vocal gestures that say "I care."

Repeated experiments show that a cute or flippant opening line is perceived less favorably than a simple, straightforward statement. Women are measurably less tolerant than men of a stranger's awkward attempts to be funny.

According to a *Parade* magazine poll, saying "Hi" works 71 percent of the time for men and 100 percent of the time for women.

Talk About What You Both Can See

The best opening lines in courtship invoke a principle of *shared focus*. In a museum, an unacquainted couple viewing a Picasso may talk about the artwork they both can see. Since they relate to something external, apart from themselves, the conversation will not seem invasive or overly personal. In the early stages of partnership, it's safer to relate indirectly to what you both see, hear, smell, or feel—"out there"—than to address each other personally as a twosome. "Who's your favorite artist?" is not the best thing to say to a stranger.

QUIZ: YOUR BEST OPENING LINE

You are sipping a latte in your favorite coffee bar. An attractive person seated nearby is typing on a laptop. You smile; a smile is returned. What's your best opening line? (Check one)

> A. "Do you live around here?" (   )
> B. "Have I seen you here before?" (   )
> C. "What kind of laptop is that?" (   )

Since it puts the focus squarely on "you," the first opening line is too personal. The second line is also too personal, with its presumption about "us." The third is just right, with a shared focus that safely points to "it," the laptop. By skirting the relationship issue—sidestepping "you and me"—C is your best opening line.

Even the best opening lines are risky. A successful pairing needs some prefacing, wordless dialogue from the Recognition Phase to take hold. Did he turn toward me as I walked by? Did her shoulders lift when I glanced at her? Did his eyes widen when he looked at me? "Cold" greetings—words spoken before receiving an eyebrow flash of recognition or an inviting shoulder shrug—may be coolly met with lowered eyebrows, a cold shoulder, or a curt reply. Encouraging signs beforehand suggest that he or she will respond. When your opening line unlocks the door to a conversation, the interview has just begun. In Phase Three, body language matters more than ever.

Move Your Hands

For success in the Conversation Phase, move your hands. Like e-mailed emoticons, gestures add emotion to words. Hand gestures show conviction, engage listeners personally, and lend credibility to verbal remarks. A hand moved toward your partner's body brings you closer together in space. Studies find that without hand gestures, words are less dramatic, less expressive, less interesting, less believable, and harder to comprehend.

> While speaking, reach your hand out to draw listeners in.

Your most attractive hand gesture is the universally friendly *palm-up* sign. Partners are more attentive—and you present a friendlier image—when you reach out with an open hand. The gesture seems to say "Here, I give you my word." Like reaching out to shake hands, a palm show promises goodwill and invites approach.

Unsightly palms, digits, and fingernails interfere with the hand's ability to communicate. A soiled or negative appearance diverts attention from expressive hand shapes and gestures. From research on "The Language of Hands," we learned that subjects were less able to read and decode gestures made with physically distressed hands. Jagged nails, dirty palms, prominent wrinkles, dry skin, chapped knuckles, visible calluses, age spots, scars, stains, and other unkempt physical traits detract from what your hand movements "say." Since gestures enhance comprehension of words, speakers with poorly groomed hands appear less fluent than speakers whose hands are regularly maintained. For best results in the Conversation Phase, put your best hands forward.

W e respond to gestures with an extreme alertness and, one might almost say, in accordance with an elaborate and secret code that is written nowhere, known by none, and understood by all.

—Edward Sapir (1927:556).

FIELD NOTES: TÊTE-À-TÊTE AT 40,000 FEET

"Saturday P.M., Nov. 23—Aboard Southwest Airlines flight 358, Oakland to San Diego," my field notes read. I was sitting behind a forty-year-old man in a pilot's uniform ("Bill") and his twenty-five-year-old seatmate ("Jen"), who wore her silky blonde hair straight and long. Seat 11-F in their row had been removed for emergency-exit access, giving a clear view of the right side of her body in 11-E and a partial view of his in 11-D. I could see neither faces nor eyes as they buckled their seatbelts, but from bobbing heads, bubbling voices, and laughter, I recognized courtship—opening Phase Three.

"What do you do?" Bill asked with a head nod. I watched the tops of his ears redden, signaling the onset of a blush. Before asking, the pilot had turned his shoulders and face around to his right to align with hers. (Jen sat on his right.) As he posed the question, Bill leaned toward her, bringing his face six inches closer.

"I work in real estate," Jen replied with a perky nod of her head. As she answered, Jen leaned away to her right; their faces were six inches farther apart again. She compensated for his "forward" lean with a backward lean of her own. The pilot's face had

CONTINUED ON NEXT PAGE

crossed an invisible boundary line, and she retreated but not entirely. As Jen leaned away, she brought her upper body around to square with his. The leftward twist of her spine above her knees, which were crossed and angled right, created an ambivalent "pretzel" posture—a display of approach and avoidance I had seen before. She engaged him with her torso, but held her legs in check.

Responding to Jen's lean away, Bill returned his head to its normal upright and locked position above his shoulders. He kept facing her but no longer leaned in, and the conversation went on unabated. Jen, who spoke, continued to lean away, with the small of her back pressed against the right armrest now behind her. For the next five minutes from this position, with her head an arm's length from his—as Bill gave his undivided attention by returning her gaze, lifting his eyebrows in response, and head-nodding with her in synchrony—Jen emitted a barrage of Conversation Phase cues to invite him closer.

Jennifer launched a series of hair preens. She reached her right hand up and all the way over her left ear, pulled tresses backward off her left cheek, and jerked her head upward to the left at Bill. Jen's hair preens and head-tossing movements invited him with their conspicuous movements: "Look at me." As Bill spoke, she flexed and raised her sweater-clad shoulders to signal "Move closer." When she answered one of his questions with "If I marry . . . ," Jen opened, raised, extended, and displayed her right palm as if to say, "I'm available."

The flight continued smoothly after drinks were served. Jen repeated her hair preens, head tosses, shoulder shrugs, and palm shows. Bill leaned closer again. Jen's body acted out its moods in clear tones, and Bill responded in kind. Eventually, Jen shifted in her seat and brought her left shoulder closer to Bill's right arm. She tilted her head over, left, closer to his head. He tilted his head right, closer to hers. As we began our descent into Lindbergh Field, Bill and Jen sat shoulder-to-shoulder, their heads two inches away. The conversation continued in slower and softer tones. Redness faded from Bill's ears. In the span of an hour and twenty minutes, the courtship of Jen and Bill evolved from talking to touching as they hugged in the jetway after the flight.

Good Timing

As they speak in the Conversation Phase, couples establish an essential synchrony that could carry them forward to lovemaking and to the pair bond following in its wake. Those who study the coordinated movements and postures of *conversational synchrony* decode them as "messages of intimacy" (Burgoon, 1994:256). Moving hands in time with a partner's hands, head-nodding rhythmically together, and taking coordinated, well-paced speaking turns without awkward pauses signal that your relationship has shifted into a higher gear.

Courtship needs more than faces, figures, and opening lines; it needs timing. Nowhere is timing more crucial than in how partners synchronize their speaking and listening turns. To begin a turn, the speaker generally looks away from the listener and closes by looking back. A rising intonation at the end of a sentence gives permission for the listener to speak. Then, when the latter's hand drops after gesturing, the partner gets another turn. Visible and audible signals tell when to speak and when to listen. Speaking out of turn shows inattention to nonverbal cue. Like a miscue in dance, inattention may lead to stepping on a partner's toes.

In the United States, long pauses are similarly painful. GSR studies show that couples become anxious as speech falters and gives way to stillness (Cappella, 1983). Silence upsets the conversational rhythm and interferes with rapport. There are cultural differences to take into account. Pausing is less likely to upset a partner from China or Japan. Asian cultures are more tolerant of quiet periods in the Conversation Phase.

Unable to speak, animals synchronize their body movements in courtship much as we do. Like us, reptiles, mammals, and birds synchronize to show they are on the same wavelength before mating. Mallards push their heads up and pull them down with a jerk, in rhythmic "head-pumping" gestures usually begun by the female. The drake faces the nodding hen and moves his head up and down in syncopated rhythm with hers. Like human beings, ducks dance in synchrony to couple as one.

Like birds of a feather, Bill and Jen head-nodded in synchrony on their flight to San Diego. To a herpetologist, their head movements would resemble those of the green anole lizard. A female anole gives the same puppetlike head-bobbing gestures to a male that she expects to receive from him. Eventually, he picks up her rhythm, and they bob in unison. Bettyann Kevles describes anole courtship in her book *Females of the Species*: "The female's peculiar posture toward the male, and his toward her, contributes to building up the synchrony between them that is the height of courtship" (1986:55–6). While the intellectual gap between reptiles and humans is immense, in courtship there is practically no gap at all.

A way to build synchrony in the workplace is to "walk the talk." Since office workers have fixed, daily routines, it's easy to intercept a colleague on walkabout to lunch. Walking ties you together psychologically as fellow travelers. You go in the same direction, follow the same pathway, and share the same sights and sounds en route. The two-point rhythm of bipedal striding synchronizes your bodies and joins your minds. Since they're controlled by the same oscillatory spinal-cord circuits that moved the forelimbs of quadrupedal ancestors, your arms rhythmically swing together as you walk side by side. Walking and talking together, your bodies join in a dance.

For best results, walk on a partner's left side and speak into the left ear. The left ear is more in tune with emotions than the logic-minded right ear, which is cerebral and analytic. The left ear picks up subtle keys and musical notes in voice *prosody*. Hearing words without their melody, the right ear processes literal meanings but misses emotions nuanced in "feelings."

Walking together, you relax and relate without the strain of eye contact. You face ahead rather than face each other head-on. In doing so, you become what philosophers call *peripatetics*. The followers of Aristotle were known as peripatetics because, instead of sitting in place, they walked and talked to share ideas. Bipedal rhythms in their strolls promoted comradeship, enhanced creativity, and cleared the mind. Peripatetic couples feel closer in courtship as well, as they converse on hiking trails, city sidewalks, and garden paths. Sharing the same pathway paves the way for a deeper meeting of minds.

When Primate Eyes Meet

Simon LeVay, neurobiologist and author of *The Sexual Brain*, writes that eye contact plays a unique role in the courtship of primates. We ourselves are primates, for whom gaze is singularly important. Studies suggest that you can boost your attractiveness quotient simply by looking into another's eyes. Whether your face is comely or plain, a direct gaze combined with smiling, brow-raising, and spontaneity can make you better looking by raising your level of "perceived attractiveness" (Burgoon, 1994:251).

In people, monkeys, and apes, eye contact and facial cues are received in dedicated vision centers of the temporal lobes. From there, sensory impressions travel downward to the *hypothalamus*, a brain structure about the size of a thumbnail, which plays a key role in sexual behavior.

Next to human beings, LeVay notes, marmosets—small, clawed, New World monkeys—give and receive the most eye contact in courtship. Initially, a female marmoset stares at a male. If, and only if, the male returns her gaze for several seconds, does she take the next step in the courting sequence, rapid tongue-flicking between the lips. When he returns her tongue-flicking cue, mounting takes place (LeVay, 1993).

In the Conversation Phase, eye-to-eye contact does not lead as quickly to sexual contact as it does in marmosets. Nonetheless, eye contact may be a prerequisite. Our brain's vision centers and hypothalamus are essentially the same as those in other primates. For humans, the link between mutual gaze and sexual arousal can be strong enough to prompt "love at first sight." A single glance may spark intense desire.

Studies in Western societies reveal that women gaze longer at partners than men do. A man should not assume that a woman's lengthy gaze-holding is anything more than politeness. In a conversation, her eye contact does not mean the same thing as a marmoset's, despite what he may wish. Nor should he suppose that a woman who stands "close" to talk, shows heightened interest. Studies agree that, compared to men, women adopt more intimate conversational distances with males and females alike. These gender differences sometimes cause confusion.

A way to test a man's interest in the Conversation Phase is to calculate the ratio of eye contact he gives while speaking to what he gives while listening. Studies suggest that, compared to women, men are more "visually dominant." That is, men give more eye contact while speaking than while listening. Men dominate listeners with their eyes, then withhold gaze as they themselves listen. But in courtship, things change. Men give enraptured eye contact to women they like, even while listening. Like Bill the pilot and his animal counterpart, the male marmoset, a smitten man cannot turn away.

A basic finding about eyes in relationships is that "gaze begets gaze." In controlled experiments, subjects averted their eyes, angled their upper bodies away, and leaned back from interviewers who did not look at them, significantly more than they did with interviewers who gazed directly into their eyes. Whether agreeing or disagreeing, as the interviewer gave more eye contact, the interviewee gazed and smiled more (Cappella, 1983). In courtship the implication is clear: Look or be overlooked.

Reading Eye Movements

In conversation, eyes move as if they had minds of their own. The six muscles that cooperate to move each eyeball are ancient and common to all vertebrates. Since nerves controlling the six muscles link to unconscious as well as to thinking parts of the human brain, eyes can disclose otherwise hidden expectations and moods.

To decipher unvoiced thoughts, watch for CLEMs. CLEM, the acronym for *conjugate lateral eye movement*, is a nonverbal response to a verbal question. In answering, your partner will make a telling eye movement away to the right or left side. A CLEM is an involuntary shift to one side only. Both eyes switch to the right in tandem, or both switch to the left. The irises rest for one or two seconds at the eye corners before centering again, to signal momentary information processing, indecision, or doubt.

To decipher unvoiced thoughts, watch for CLEMs.

Neurologically, CLEM movements are an index of brain-hemispheric activation. They show something is going on upstairs that has not been put into words—and perhaps never will be. Your date may disagree without saying so, or dissent without telling you why. Psychologists estimate that three out of four people are exclusively "right lookers" or "left lookers," while the rest look either way (Richmond et al., 1991).

In courtship, CLEMs reveal doubt. If you ask "Would you like to have dinner tonight?" and see a CLEM, your invitation may be problematic or premature. Test the CLEM with a verbal probe: "Would tomorrow be better?" Another CLEM means it's not yet time for a serious dinner date. A light lunch may be better.

To look good, look up the muscle that lifts your upper eyelid, *levator palpebrae superioris*, arose from *superior rectus*, one of the six muscles that rotate the eyeball itself. Since their connective tissue coats are fused, you automatically lift your eyelids when you look up. In a conversation lifted lids appeal and beckon for notice. When you tip your face slightly downward and gaze up at your partner, your eyes open wider and your lashes prominently show.

More Ways to Read Lips

To assess your partner's moods, watch the mouth corners. Sudden onset of an unhappy mood is visible in down-turned lips. A droopy mouth means you've said something wrong or suggests that a disturbing thought—perhaps unrelated to you—has entered your partner's mind. The downward shift in lip corners signals a downward shift in mood.

In momentary sadness, an emotional muscle, *depressor anguli oris*, pulls the mouth corners down. When this muscle contracts, only the corners lower. It is not a grief-stricken expression but a mildly unhappy frown. *Mini frowns* are easily overlooked, but the emotions behind them should not be. A mini frown explicitly reveals when something is wrong. When you see lips pull down for longer than a few seconds, probe to learn if the expression pertains to you. Read lips to see if the mood is right before moving ahead to the Touch Phase.

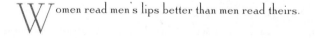

Women read men's lips better than men read theirs.

Women can read men's lips better than men can read theirs. For decades, studies have shown that women have slightly higher verbal skills and significantly higher nonverbal skills than men. Eighty-four percent of sixty-one studies conclude that women are better at deciphering emotions from body-language cues (Manstead, 1998). Since she reads his motives before he reads hers, a woman is likely to be the first to break away from an unsatisfactory conversation, or be the first to touch. That she has superior skills in the Conversation Phase means she decides.

In conversations, women smile more. They are more expressive facially and vocally than men (Burgoon, 1994). Women are more likely to smile "on purpose" to get acquainted with unfamiliar men (LaFrance and Hecht, 2000).

Words in the Right Key

Couples research has shown that listeners are likely to judge you more physically attractive when you speak in a pleasant tone of voice (Gross and Crofton, 1977). In right-handed listeners, the left-brain hemisphere hears words while the right brain hears their melody. In Phase Three, your best speaking voice sounds softer, more musical, and more yielding than it sounds in a normal conversation with friends.

Throat, larynx, and pharynx muscles are controlled by the same special visceral nerves linked to the muscles of facial expression. Tone of voice reflects emotional feelings as precisely and faithfully as lip, brow, and eye movements. Anxiety is evident, for instance, as throat muscles constrict to produce a strained, raspy voice. The muscles tense to seal off the throat and protect the alimentary canal from harm.

Devoid of inflection, a monotonal voice sounds unenthusiastic and bored. A loud voice sounds domineering and pushy. A tense voice sounds frustrated, angry, and rude. In courtship a softer, higher-pitched voice—the voice adults use with young children and pets—communicates an attitude of parental caring. Its lighthearted tenor is cheerful, calming, and universally friendly. Use the light voice to sound like you care.

V oice tones are contagious in courtship. Yours should be worth catching.

Where You Talk Matters

When getting to know someone new, a spacious room is better than a smaller room or private office. From GSR experiments psychologists have learned that, when in the company of strangers, smaller spaces arouse more anxiety than larger ones (Cappella, 1983). Roominess feels better, presumably because at some point we may need to flee.

In a roomful of people, it's easier to hear a woman's voice against a background of men speaking. For hearing the voice of a man, the converse is true. Human factors research shows that physically similar voices cancel each other out. By strategically choosing an area occupied mostly by men, a woman makes it easy for partners to hear her lighter voice against deeper masculine sounds (Kantowitz and Sorkin, 1983).

The most sociable places to talk offer readily available food items. Drinks and appetizers arouse appetites for sociability and talk. Chips, crackers, and meatballs on toothpicks are bondworthy "finger foods." Frontal-lobe areas that control our finger movements border cerebral centers in charge of speech. The manual dexterity required to dip a chip stimulates the articulatory circuits required for chat. Neurologically, they go hand in hand. Since breaking bread together enlivens talk, eating areas are typically talkative.

Hot Topics

In conversations, we are drawn to people who agree with us. A woman finds a man more physically and sexually attractive, research shows, when he asks for her opinion, shows sensitivity to her ideas, and displays overall warmth and agreeableness. Men, too, rate agreeable women as the "most attractive and desirable" dates.

For women, cross-cultural studies identify the "most appealing" men as those who talk about their ambitions, industriousness, and positive financial prospects. This resonates with a theme in the courtship of animals known as *provisioning*. Males who display the ability to provide for females by offering protection or sharing food are more likely to win their affection as mates.

In our own courtship, psychologist David Buss believes, women have been programmed by millions of years of evolution to prefer mates who show potential to provide food, protection, and other resources. From his six-continent study of 10,047 people in thirty-seven cultures, Buss found that women place high value on a man's ambition and education (Buss, 1998). For men, talking about career goals in a fancy restaurant is a proven way to connect. Footing the bill proves a man's evolutionary worth.

> The sound of a woman's voice activates a man's left temporal lobe. The sound of a man's voice engages her right and left temporal lobes. She listens with two sides of her brain; he listens with half.

"Nothing is often a good thing to do," historian Will Durant wrote, "and always a good thing to say." But in courtship, you need to say something or the partner will go away. Speaking establishes synchrony, engenders rapport, and when spoken in the right key, makes you sound caring, empathetic, and attractive.

In the Conversation Phase, you communicate verbally and nonverbally at the same time. Research shows that when speech and body language are simultaneous, nonverbal cues dominate. In fact, body language can be twelve times as powerful as speech. When partners receive mixed messages, they turn to body language for the truth. For the sake of credibility in courtship, the words you say and the way you say them must be congruent. If you are credible, you may move on to courtship's next level, the Touch Phase.

5. PHASE FOUR:
THE LANGUAGE OF TOUCH

Not only our geometry and physics, but our
whole conception of what exists outside us, is based
upon the sense of touch.
—BERTRAND RUSSELL

COUPLES WHO ESTABLISH proper romantic synchrony in a conversation—hold each other's eyes, laugh in unison, head-nod in agreement, hair-preen in tandem, and appeal with opened palms—are destined to reach out and touch. In Phase Four, we transcend the logic of talking and communicate in a more persuasive tactile mode. Millions of years older than words, touch cues encode a primordial sense of closeness. Gentle pats, playful bites, embraces, tickles, nuzzles, and kisses pave the way for life's greatest tactile experience, lovemaking.

The skin is our largest sense organ, making up 15 percent of body weight, about 23 pounds, and occupying 21 square feet of surface area. Touch is the second oldest sensory organ, after smell. What we touch is more concrete than what we see or hear. The most active and exploratory sense, touch convinces our brain beyond a doubt that something is *real.*

In courtship, only the ancient language of touch can reassure that the ultimate closeness, sexual intercourse, will be all right. Before making love, we gently handle each other to be sure.

Not just any touch will serve. The best tactile cues—the kiss, the caress, the handhold—come from the mother-infant bond. Like baby monkeys, we need a mother's touch to function properly as adults. We touch lovers softly, as mothers caress babies, for sound evolutionary reasons. Just as enamored elephants intertwine their trunks, and wooing whales nuzzle, we touch to stimulate the caring—and to simulate the harmlessness—of infancy. Through the tactile channel, we become each other's baby.

Maternal touching permeates animal courtship as it does our own. Elephants caress. Chimpanzees hug, kiss, and pat. Baboons and jackals groom. Possums and lions lick. Touching and licking tame the beast by bringing out the harmless infant—and by stimulating infant-care attitudes in the adult animal at the same time.

In human courtship, touch has deeper meanings than speech. When someone touches your sensitive, nearly hairless body, that person has your complete attention. Touch is a narrower, more exclusive channel for communication, and the meaning of a tactile cue is more emotionally charged. A soft, stroking movement of fingertips on the nape of the neck bypasses thinking parts of the brain and cuts directly to feelings. What's more, the person touched will either like or dislike the signal immediately, because touching evokes a clear "yes-or-no" reaction. The response is either positive or negative and rarely ever neutral.

To grasp the magic of touching, we shall decipher the language of hands. Hands are the tactile antennae we throw out to assay the material world and to palpate its moods. Most of the twenty kinds of nerve fiber in each hand fire off simultaneously, sending orders to muscles and glands or receiving touch, motion, and position information from sense organs embedded in tendons, muscles, and skin (Amato, 1992).

Our fingers show emotion, depict ideas, and point to butterflies on the wing. They read Braille, speak in sign languages, and write poetry. There is no better organ than a hand for gauging courtship's unspoken thoughts, feelings, and moods.

Courtship begins to move faster with the first touch. It may move too fast, couples report. The tactile mode exerts a tidal pull toward completion. The shift from vision and hearing to touching brings courtship to primal circuits of the cerebrum and brain stem. Control shifts downward to primitive neural centers, the mute authority of which verges on the dictatorial. With hands laid on, courtship gets out of hand as the heart runs away with the head.

> I recently ran into an old friend from high school. In the course of our ten-minute "what-have-you-been-up-to" conversation, she touched my elbow three or four times. Later that evening when I told a buddy about the incident, he said (and I quote), "What are you doing here? You should be having sex with her right now!"
>
> The point of the story is that seemingly "random" physical contact is an indicator of romantic interest. It's interesting, I think, because sometimes it seems like a conscious move and sometimes it seems unconscious. I find it fascinating that we feel free to express ourselves through body language about things we would never speak of in words.
>
> —Matt

Touch Lightly the Brain

The best touches in courtship are light, like a cotton ball or feather drawn against the palm. A gentle caress registers in nerves, called *C-fibers*, that detect pleasurable sensations to the skin. C-fibers are more "emotional" than faster-conducting A-fibers, which pick up sensations of pressure, roughness, and dryness. The latter respond to the details of touch; the former respond to pleasure.

A gentle caress registers in nerves, called *C-fibers*, that detect pleasurable sensations to the skin.

We find pleasure in touching a partner's soft shoulders. Smoothness stimulates tactile sensations for the "light touch." Merely seeing a bared shoulder can tease the tactile response. The pleasurable sense of light touch runs through evolutionary-old pathways to sensual centers of the emotional brain, including the *cingulate gyrus* and *frontal cortex*.

A tender touch to the face is arousing. Tactile messages travel through *trigeminal nerves*, which carry impulses from the impressionable skin of the cheeks, lips, and forehead to the brain. The feel of another's fingertips pushing hair from your forehead is sensual. A kiss to your upper lip stimulates specialized whiskers called *vibrissae*. Thicker in men, vibrissae are incredibly responsive to touch because they evolved as mammalian feelers. Nerve endings attached to these touch-sensitive hairs can make a kiss feel ticklish and tingly.

The entire *perioral area*, which includes your lips, nose, and immediately surrounding skin, is sensitive to touch cues. It responds to "serious" touches in courtship, like the Eskimo-style nose rub, the New Guinea lip bite, and the worldwide lip-to-lip kiss. Since it stimulates three cranial nerves at once—the *facial, glossopharyngeal,* and *vagal*—gently blowing in your partner's ear is arousing as well.

Touch cues delivered by fingertips to hairless (or *glabrous*) areas of skin—to the palms of the hands and soles of the feet—are similarly exciting. The brain's master switching station, the *thalamus*, routes their sensations directly to pleasure centers of the mammalian brain. The fact that toes and genital organs are next-door neighbors on the brain's sensory strip, located on the *parietal lobe*, makes foot-rubbing a provocative ploy in courtship.

MRI studies show that light touches to the hand activate the brain's emotional *orbitofrontal cortex*. Stronger touches activate the brain's *sensory cortex*, a less emotional area. For maximum effect, touching should be gentle. When you caress a partner's inner forearm, tactile impulses travel through C-fibers to stimulate pleasurable itching, tickling, and sexual sensations.

With right-handed partners, target the body's left-hand side. The left side of the body communicates with the right side of the brain. Superior fiber linkages in the right-brain hemisphere connect to feelings, senses, and memories, and give the left side of the body its deeper-reaching nonverbal skills.

Another type of light touch is tickling. Used by parents and children around the world to show playful affection, tickling is commonplace in courtship as well. The English word *tickle* comes from Middle English *tikelen*: "to touch lightly." Tickling brings out the child with its innocent, "unserious" touches to the body.

The two tickle types are *knismesis*, a light tickle that may or may not produce laughter, and *gargalesis*, a heavy tickle that produces a laugh. Laughter releases the euphoria-promoting brain chemicals endorphin, enkephalin, and dopamine. Mutual laughter from tickling strengthens emotional ties. By stimulating nonspecific erogenous areas of a partner's skin, tickling the neck, armpits, and sides of the abdomen stir sexual feelings.

The left wrist, left arm, left shoulder, and left ear respond more passionately to tactile contact than their counterparts on the right. You should usually touch left, unless your partner is left-handed, then touch right.

The First Touch

The first touch is an emotional milestone. It is likely to seem "accidental" rather than serious. A woman reaches over a man's shoulder for her coat, extends herself a bit too far, and grasps his shoulder to steady herself. An open hand reaches for a neutral body part—a forearm or wrist—which reacts by accepting the contact or by pulling away.

Supersensitive tactile pads of your fingertips gauge the slightest startle, tenseness, or hesitation of response. You learn a great deal from the first touch, which deftly probes beneath spoken words to feelings. Touching another's body captures full attention and is the true test of where a partner stands.

How do couples manage their first touch? In very public places like theaters, restaurants, and bars, men and women may defer touching and handle a *body extension* instead. A body extension is, according to Edward Hall, the anthropologist who coined the term, a purse, glove, or briefcase—anything a person holds or wears to supplement the body's natural endowments.

Body extensions, Hall suggests, mark personality as hands, arms, and body parts themselves do. In effect, we "rub off" onto our possessions. Handling a woman's purse or pen makes personal contact without actually touching the skin. Handling a man's notebook or cell phone hints at the likely next step, touching his hand. In courtship, touching body extensions is a "hedge" because owners cannot feel the contact. Yet they react as if you'd touched the skin itself. How they respond—with interest or apathy—suggests how they might react to a true touch.

One way to invite touch is to handle jewelry. A man communicates his unspoken wish to touch by feigning interest in a woman's bracelet or wristwatch. She may have worn the eye-catching timepiece deliberately to send a "touch me" message. He spans his index finger and thumb around her wristwatch and comments on its design. In courtship, touching a ring, necklace, pendant, or pin is the same—a hedged first touch. Handle an accessory and note the response. Does she lean in or pull away? Does he smile or tighten his lips?

As a visible message, reaching an open hand outward is appealing. Open palms was a favorite gesture of Ray Birdwhistell, the anthropologist who founded *kinesics* (the scientific study of body language). In experiments, Birdwhistell rotated both hands upward and reached them out to strangers as he spoke. He was delighted to learn that nearly everyone had the same reaction. Invited to touch, most responded and placed their palms atop his.

So appealing is the palm show that it works even with nonhuman primates. A classic example is "Peanuts," the mountain gorilla who gently touched primatologist Dian Fossey's hand with his own. In 1970, Dian hesitantly extended her open palm to Peanuts in a remote African rainforest. He responded and became the first wild gorilla to "hold hands" with a human being.

A TELLTALE REACH IN THE CROCODILE

A man may telegraph his desire to touch merely by stretching his arms toward a woman. Biologists call the unwitting reach, which shows a partial movement toward a goal, an *intention cue*. I observed a dramatic intention to "reach out and touch someone" at the Crocodile Café, a Gen-X nightspot for cocktails and rock music in Seattle. Amy and her boyfriend, Rick, both in their twenties, sat together at a 4-foot round table, enjoying the music and sipping Manhattans. Their noses were 18 inches apart.

Amy's friend Ben joined and sat across from the pair. After some introductory chitchat, Rick excused himself to go out for a smoke and left Ben and Amy alone. Abruptly, the conversation came alive with head-bobbing movements, gaze-holding, and laughter. Then, with the poise of a method actor, Ben bent

CONTINUED ON NEXT PAGE

forward at the waist, lay his chest against the tabletop, and stretched his arms toward Amy. In response, she leaned forward, put both elbows on the table, and rested her chin in her palms. Their noses were 12 inches apart.

From my vantage point at the Crocodile, I could not hear the words, but their body language told a story. Ben's prostrate pose on the table was submissive. His prone body strained in Amy's direction, showing he was strongly attracted but unlikely to pressure her or overstep his bounds.

Ben kept both arms extended as if "reaching" across the table. He flipped his right palm up as he spoke. Amy touched the back of Ben's left hand, which he'd placed palm down on the table, with a series of fingertip pats. She met his invitation to touch with literal touches of her own. When Rick returned from his cigarette break, the trio sat upright as they had before. The five-minute courtship was over, at least for the moment. Later that night, Amy left the Crocodile with Ben.

In courtship, the first touch is a test. Like a stethoscope over a heart, skin-to-skin contact gives an accurate reading of mood. Overall, people respond favorably to a brief touch to a sexually neutral body part. A pat on the back of a hand, wrist, or forearm engenders rapport and lets you take the partner's pulse. A limb that advances when touched is palpably friendlier than one that retreats.

In the beginning, avoid touching a partner's head. People instinctively flinch as fingers reach toward their face and eyes. The *flexion withdrawal response* is among the most primitive of all protective reflexes. Unauthorized contact with a forehead, ear, cheek, or neck evokes pulling away, a negative reaction. Equally unsuitable are chests, hips, thighs, and bottoms. They are sexually loaded in all cultures. Cheeks, hips, and thighs are for later in courtship's progression.

For a man, the small of a woman's back—the spinal area between her shoulder blades and waist—is a good place to touch. Use the *back-assist* to guide her through a doorway or a crowded room. The gesture connotes self-assurance with a subtle undertone of sexuality. *Cosmopolitan* magazine ranks the back-assist as one of a man's "100 Most Compelling" sexual signs.

T ouch yourself to seem more touchable.

As a woman, touching your own body invites a man to do the same. The principle of isopraxism comes into play. Massaging the back of your hand, wrist, or forearm—better yet, rubbing your shoulder, a more expressive body part—connotes that you would like him to touch as well. A woman's body language is more sensual than that of a man. Self-touching sparks an intimacy that is contagious. Touching yourself says that you yourself are touchable.

Self-touching cues—in this case, hand-to-cheek and thumb-to-arm—suggest "I am touchable."

We human beings are very imitative primates. "Monkey see, monkey do" is more than a saying; it's a biological fact. Just as chimpanzees solicit a grooming session by grooming themselves, we massage our own bodies to appeal for touch. The compulsion to imitate comes from the primate brain's cingulate gyrus, a cortical area programmed with motivational software designed to promote the grooming of the young.

The best place for a first touch is the back of a hand or the topside of a forearm. Since the palm is unusually sensitive to pressure, vibration, and the pleasurable light touch, touching palmar skin is too "personal." Since the forearm's underside has heightened sensitivity to body heat, a touch there is too "intimate." And since emotionally sensitive nerves control the shoulders, they are too "excitable" for first contact. Touch rougher areas of skin on the dorsal side of a hand, wrist, or forearm to avoid setting off an alarm bell.

Many courtships begin with a handshake. A widespread greeting ritual, handshaking is a culturally acceptable way to touch another's palm. While an introductory shake may not lead to further touching, it helps set the stage. Begin your handshake with a moderately firm clasp (not as strong as the business shake), followed by a more relaxed grip to test the softness and warmth of your partner's skin. For an emotionally "yielding" handshake, rotate your palm a few degrees upward and over to the right. The submissive twist gives your partner the "upper hand" and grants permission to hold hands longer.

As a tactile signal, a cold or damp palm due to stranger anxiety is not as damaging as you think. People do not perceive lack of hand warmth as a negative sign. Cool palms signal shyness, and in the early stages of a relationship, shyness is becoming. Biologists have documented a widespread aversion to physical contact in the courtship of animals. From wolves to monkeys to cats, animals instinctively emit fear signals before touching a mate. Timidity shows they are not likely to become aggressive. In humans, cool palms reflect a natural reserve that appeals more than overconfidence.

MEN HANDLE, WOMEN FEEL

Men and women hold mismatched views of what it means to touch and be touched. They reach out to each other as if to different species.

In the early stages of a relationship, men are more likely to touch than women. Women, studies confirm, are more comfortable touching later on (Canary and Emmers-Sommer, 1997). A man may reach out with a proprietary touch to express sexual interest or to show that a woman belongs to him. At the least, his firm clasp about her waist or shoulders tests the proposition.

A man decodes the first touch as a sexual sign. "She touched me, therefore she wants me," the masculine mind concludes. But the logic is faulty, because a woman's first touch is not as pointedly sexual as that of a man. Instead, it demonstrates her feeling about the overall warmth, inclusiveness, and comfort level of a relationship. She may enjoy the closeness of the moment for its own sake—not as a lead-in to physical sex. Her kinder, gentler pats reflect a feeling of empathy, support, and connectedness. A touch by the male of our species, on the other hand, reflects little more than sexuality.

As a woman, you may ask, "How can I tell if he's interested in me or just wants to be friends?" The answer lies in how often he touches. Studies show that women touch more and seek more physical contact in relationships than men do. In courtship, the roles are reversed, and men touch significantly more. When a woman gets more than the usual number of pats, brushes, and tickles from a friend, he wants to be more than friends.

A man should know that a "relationship touch" to his hand, wrist, or forearm has little to do with sex. A woman should know that a man's sexual touch to her waist, neck, or shoulder says little about his emotional involvement or willingness to commit.

The First Embrace

The next level of touching begins with a love signal known as the *hug*. "Hug" comes from the Scandinavian word *hugga*, "to comfort." The biological roots of hugging are in fact linked to comfort and caring. Primate babies are innately programmed to cling. Functional from birth to four months, the *Moro reflex* is the human equivalent of the ancient clinging response. In times of danger, infant monkeys and apes cling to their mother's fur with an instinctively tight grasp. So firm is the clasp that newborn primates—monkeys, apes, and humans alike—can hang, unaided, from a branch or a clothesline.

Holding in the arms is a natural response to the infantile cling. Clinging, a sign of needing to be mothered, is met with holding, the universal mothering response. Embracing is the evolutionary correct way to say "I love you," and the proper primate way to say "I need you" as well. In an embrace, we rock each other gently from side to side. The swaying motion stimulates pleasure centers of the brain linked to the inner ear's vestibular sense. As we become each other's baby in courtship, rocking brings the sentiment home.

Courting couples touch as if they were each other's baby.

We use the primate hug, with very little modification, as a courting sign. Hugging shows parental affection and reassures the person who is hugged. To many, the hugging response is as important as, or even more important than, making love. This is true for the estimated 20 to 25 percent of U.S. women who are sexually inhibited. Being held produces a satisfying sense of safety, security, and comfort. Substantially more women than men crave being hugged, studies show. A woman's desire to give and receive hugs explains the curious sex appeal of large-girthed men whom we liken to "teddy bears." A man need not be thin or athletic, necessarily, only huggable.

The first embrace may come soon after the first touch. A playful pat on the back leads to an exploratory *side hug*. Your hand reaches around the partner's waist or cups the upper arm's fleshy deltoid, and your partner responds in kind. As you stand side by side, with hips almost touching, you give two or three rhythmic squeezes to pull each other closer.

Side hugs are playful and seemingly noncommittal. Indeed, almost every signal up to this point has been playful, mischievous, and light. The joking quality of early touching reveals that sincere commitment is not quite there. Since playfulness and laughter provide an escape hatch, you can still back out gracefully. You touch, but not in a serious way—at least not yet.

Then something comes over your relationship that can only be described as a "serious hush." You join in your first *frontal embrace*, and courtship begins to move faster. When you put your arms around each other, lay your palms flat against the partner's back, and press your torsos and hips together, you have moved perilously close to lovemaking.

A front hug communicates caring and warmth and gives the first tantalizing experience of whole-body closeness. With the full frontal hug you begin to exchange leisurely embraces behind closed doors or in the privacy of hallways—away from the crowd. There is a major shifting of gears: Courtship accelerates while the speed of body movements slows.

Smiles fade and lips part. Eyelids droop in a dreamy, half-closed position called *bedroom eyes*. In some cases, partners raise and lower their eyebrows, activate both sets of competing musculature—lift with *frontalis*, pull down with *corrugator*—at the same time. Charles Darwin called this forehead seemingly at cross-purposes with itself the "grief" look. When attraction becomes irresistible, you see painfully tangled creases above the brows. Locked in a frontal embrace, you synch into a slower, more leisurely tempo, the speed you eventually move at while making love.

The First Kiss

From the hug position you are nearer to Phase Five, Making Love, than either may imagine. Sensing the seriousness of what's to come, you move away from others. Around the world, privacy is the norm. When bedrooms or motor vehicles are unavailable, there is what anthropologists call the "bush tryst." In simple societies like the Gahuku Gama of New Guinea, couples meet in the bushes to hug, kiss, and physically act out their vows.

At first, a couple's lips caress each other's cheeks. Then, by mutual consent, probing lips find their way to waiting lips through a sideward "searching" motion. This head-turning to the right or left resembles a baby's instinctive *rooting* movements across its mother's breast in search of the nipple. The first lip-to-lip kiss is the most precise test yet of a couple's ability to harmonize, to establish the essential synchrony needed for lovemaking.

From the frontal embrace, with its swaying motion to reassure that everything will be okay, faces gradually square into alignment. Eye-to-eye, nose-to-nose, heads six inches apart, your eyes lock onto your partner's in the universal *en face* that says "I love you." Peering from inches away, your partner's eyes seem to merge into one. Already sealed off from others in the hug, and spatially removed as well, you see a single, oversized eye in a corona of skin. Your exclusiveness is now complete; you and your partner are all that exists. "It's just you and me now" is more than a cliché, it's a sensory truth.

Ever so slowly, your heads loom closer. Three inches away and closing, faces roll several degrees right or left, in synchrony, so the noses will clear. And the lips begin a cautious linkup. You seal together in the first kiss.

SEALS OF LOVE

Defined scientifically according to Dr. Henry Gibbons, a kiss is "the anatomical juxtaposition of two *orbicularis oris* muscles in a state of contraction." A kiss, of course, is more than that. In courtship, kissing is a powerful medium of communication. You press your lips against another's and feel their response to your own. The sensation of being kissed arouses neurochemical feelings of euphoria that you associate with the person in front of your face.

For some, kissing is more intimate than intercourse. Though they touch the most private body parts, prostitutes refuse to kiss. In many ways kissing is also more technical than intercourse. Good kissers know how to control the rhythm and tempo of the muscular, fleshy folds around their own mouth even as they respond to the folds of a partner. They know when to press firmly, when to press lightly, when to graze teasingly with the tongue, and when to open the mouth or keep it closed. They know how to pause, breathe, and control the flow of saliva. Good kissers enjoy a kiss while managing the technical aspects of kissing at the same time.

SPARKS

Courtship's first kiss is memorable. Shannon recalls "sparks." Shannon and Eric were looking at each other and smiling when their eyes suddenly locked. "It felt like I was floating toward him," she said. "He moved his face slowly toward mine. I got really nervous, like my stomach was vibrating. Eric put his arms around my neck. I started breathing fast and felt my lips heating up. Then our lips barely touched, and mine started tingling with little sparks of electricity. There was a tickling sensation, and I couldn't get my breath."

At the very beginning of a kiss, lips make contact without offending tongues or saliva. The first kiss is gentle to strum the pleasure-carrying C-fibers. Despite what movies show, a rough kiss registers but doesn't as effectively stir pleasure centers of the brain.

Lips make *pursing* motions, like a baby's rhythmic sucking, when they meet. Everted lips communicate passion directly through infantile pulsations. The ideal first kiss is soft, light, exploratory, and lasts from three to five seconds. Close your eyes to savor the contact. This keeps the future-oriented visual sense from interfering with a kiss's tactile immediacy.

A slow-motion film study of kissing, conducted by anthropologist Adam Kendon, reveals how a woman controls her partner with the signals she sends. To deflect his kiss, she turns her head to dodge him as he moves in, and displays an *open-mouth smile*. Showing teeth, Kendon found, is a kiss-nullifying sign. When he turns toward her again and sees a *closed-mouth smile*, he moves in and kisses.

To end the kiss she pulls her head back, protrudes her tongue in a slight tongue show, swivels her face to the side, and looks away behind her shoulder. It is all closely synchronized with cues that can mean the difference between success and failure. When the man tries to override her open-mouth smile's "brake," she considers him pushy and faces away.

The man has a few options of his own. He may rub noses with her to evoke a *dreamy face*. Seeing her eyebrows lift and her lips part without significantly exposing teeth, he leans in for another kiss. Each time they rub noses, the anthropologist observed, she gives him the dreamy face. By pushing just the right button—her nose—she doesn't bare her teeth, and he is free to kiss again.

The touch cues that you exchange now prepare you for intimate moments ahead.

Touch cues are terribly real in courtship. If seeing is believing, touching is "knowing for sure." In the Touch Phase, you overcome a partner's resistance to touch with reassuring tactile cues of your own. You negotiate the timing, rhythm, and synchrony you will need later in courtship's final phase, Lovemaking. The touch signals you exchange now prepare you for intimate moments ahead.

6. PHASE FIVE: MAKING LOVE

Sex and love are inseparable, like life and consciousness.
—D. H. LAWRENCE

Among men, sex sometimes results in intimacy;
among women, intimacy sometimes results in sex.
—DONALD SYMONS

T HE FINAL AND usually briefest period of courtship is Love-making. To make love, you communicate with tender areas of your partner's body called *erogenous zones*, such as lips, eyelids, ears, the neck, and inner thighs, then stimulate touch receptors embedded in the sexual organs directly. Nonverbal signals exchanged in this very intimate stage speak about the contingencies of relationships for women, whereas for men they speak more explicitly about sex.

Like eating and breathing, lovemaking is controlled by parts of the nervous system's ancient "visceral brain," notably the hypothalamus, the pituitary gland, and pleasure centers of the midbrain. In a multisensory dialogue full of tactile, visual, aural, olfactory, and gustatory cues, couples break through the final frontiers of intimacy to validate their love.

The nonverbal act of conjoining as one entity shapes how we reflect upon love in words. In his study of love metaphors used in everyday language, linguist Zoltan Kovecses defines the Platonic ideal of love as the unity of two complementary parts. Saying "We are one" or "She's my better half" reflects this commonly held view of love as a mutual bond between halves. First written about in Plato's *Symposium* over two thousand years ago, it is the Western belief that we are incomplete until we are loved by another.

Nonverbal Love

The meaning of love is older than the words used to define it. Love calls to us nonverbally through primeval feelings of attachment combined with primordial sexual cravings. Though attachment and desire evolved on separate pathways, both are required for meaningful lovemaking to take place.

Attachment is the wish to be close to another, to make physical contact, and to take special care of the person you love. Biologists have studied attachment psychology in human beings and in our primate relatives. Among humans, a principal finding is that lovers use the same nonverbal signs infants and mothers use to maintain their close proximity. Smiling, crying, gaze-holding, and clinging serve the biological end of keeping two partners—mother and child, or woman and man—physically together in space.

In sexual communication, women respond to nonverbal signs of caring. Asked to describe the "best sexual experience you have ever had," women skip the anatomical details men recall. A woman remembers the romance, the ambience of her setting, and the feeling of having been pampered. Men recall aspects of anatomy, the contours of a woman's body, the softness, smoothness, and warmth of her skin.

The Question of When

For both sexes, courtship's perennial question is when to make love. Around the world men generally want sex sooner than women do. Men respond to a woman's sexual overtures whether or not she sends signals showing that she cares. That women want sex later rather than sooner in a relationship is because a man's sexual overtures are not enough. Along with his obvious signs of desire, women need signs of caring.

CARING SIGNALS

You are more than a sex object when your partner:

- Holds your hand.
- Adjusts your collar, grooms your clothing, or plays with your hair.
- Doesn't lose interest after the third date if lovemaking hasn't occurred.
- Calls you the day after making love.
- Does not let eyes roam while on a date.
- Attends to your needs without being overly attentive.
- Touches your arm, shoulder, or back—but not at every opportunity.
- Doesn't make a pass on the first date.

Meaningful lovemaking is more likely when couples exchange love signals showing they care for each other. Sex researchers William Masters and Virginia Johnson cite the representative case of a twenty-six-year-old man who initially enjoyed one-night stands because no demands were attached. Later he realized something was missing: a "sense of caring about the person" (Masters, Johnson, and Kolodny, 1986:161).

> The *Redbook Report on Female Sexuality* found that women in stable relationships are three times as likely to reach orgasm as those who have a series of one-night stands.

Premarital intercourse and one-night stands are part of a culturally widespread pattern of sexual experimentation. Couples around the world form temporary unions to gain experience in lovemaking. According to anthropologists, premarital sex is most prevalent in traditional Pacific-island cultures and least common in the Arab and Muslim world. Two-thirds of the 863 societies surveyed in anthropologist Edward Murdock's *Ethnographic Atlas* have few prohibitions on sex before marriage. Among the Nuer of south Sudan, anthropologist Edward Evans-Pritchard reports that girls aged fifteen or sixteen are expected to have at least one lover in their own village, and additional lovers from neighboring villages.

In the West, Denmark may be the most permissive society. The American Midwest holds what could be the most restrictive views of premarital sex. In the United States overall, an estimated 80 percent of college men and 63 percent of college women have had premarital intercourse (Ingoldsby, 1995). "Today most people in their twenties," Masters and Johnson write, "believe that becoming sexually experienced rather than preserving virginity is an important prelude for selecting a mate" (Masters, Johnson, and Kolodny, 1986:159). For many, lovemaking is an interim phase.

Sending Sexual Cues

Two kinds of communication take place in Phase Five. *Foreplay* is sexual stimulation given and received before intercourse. Intercourse, or *coitus*, is the insertion of a male's penis into a female's vagina. *Coitus* comes from the Latin word *coire*, "to copulate" by way of Latin *copula*, to "link."

Men and women have different moods and agendas in foreplay and coitus. In lovemaking, emotional contrasts between males and females are even sharper than in the Touch Phase. When sexual world views collide, lovemaking is often less than it could be.

SEXUAL WORLDVIEW

Women and men view lovemaking in fundamentally different lights:

- Men would like eighteen sexual partners in a lifetime: women, four or five (Buss, 1998).
- Women link sex with emotional involvement; men with physical (Canary and Emmers-Sommer, 1997).
- Women's fantasies include touching and feeling; men entertain visual images of coitus itself (Rodgers, 2001).
- Women buy romance novels; men buy *Playboy.*
- Men find sexual infidelity more distressing than emotional infidelity; the reverse is true for women (Buss, 1998).
- Women react to sex with a "red light"; men act with a "green light" (Canary and Emmers-Sommer, 1997).
- When a lover is silent, men assume all is well; women assume something is wrong (Fincham et al., 1993).
- Ninety percent of men and 40 percent of women claim they reach orgasm in coitus "most of the time."

Nonverbal Signs of Orgasm

An orgasm is the brain's way of saying "Sex is wonderful," and nature's way of addicting us to love. Why else would couples willingly join in the curious act of coitus? An orgasm is not unlike the thrill of a roller coaster's initial plunge. The sudden pleasure in the "seat of your pants" happens as the brain releases a neurochemical, dopamine, and the hormone oxytocin.

Orgasm comes from the Greek word *orgasmos*, which means "swelling" or "excitement." You feel a profoundly pleasurable illumination that "glows" in the genitals and spreads through the pelvic area. There may be tingling sensations in your fingers and toes, a whole-body relaxation response, feelings of sexual release, and a sense of joyful, ecstatic depletion.

Psychologist John Money describes the experience as a "voluptuous rapture of ecstasy" that goes off simultaneously in the brain and sexual organs. It happens, he says, through intercommunication of nerve networks above and below the waist. An orgasm may be touched off physically by foreplay and coitus, or mentally by erotic thoughts and imagery. For a few, Mozart, a dozen roses, or a single kiss may trigger the response. Many roads lead to love's rapture, but studies agree that significantly fewer women than men attain it through coitus alone, principally because men do not send the right signals.

Nonverbal symptoms of orgasm include skin flushing about the face and neck, an involuntarily open mouth or jaw droop, reflexive bending and extension movements of the hands and feet, faster breathing and panting, intense muscle tension, an arched back, and whole-body spasms. Audible signs are moaning, sighing, laughing, crying, and screaming. Tactile signals include muscular contractions in the outer third of the vaginal wall, stiffening of the abdominal muscles, and rhythmic contractions in muscles around the base of the penis and vagina and in muscles of the lower pelvic area.

In this, the most physical stage of courtship, there are significant mismatches in the body language of men and women. Succinctly stated by Harvard Medical School gynecologist Elizabeth Stewart, "The penis in the vagina is not enough for most women to achieve orgasm" (Stewart, 2002:116). The Kinsey Institute has found that up to 70 percent of women do not climax from intercourse alone. And yet a man easily climaxes, because procreation depends on orgasm to propel his sperm cells to her awaiting egg.

Foreplay Cues

The body language of foreplay is remarkably the same around the world: fondling, caressing with fingertips, kissing with the lips, touching with the tongue, and an intimate form of "touch" called *love talk*.

Couples everywhere use soft voice tones to strum the inner ear's *cochlear* nerve, which evolved in early vertebrates from the sense of touch. In foreplay, love talk can be as arousing as a touch to the body itself.

A woman may respond more fervently in foreplay to touches and love talk than to a man's body movements in coitus. She may experience one or more orgasms brought on simply by his caressing hands. However, a man may not spend as much time caressing as she likes. He is genetically programmed to move beyond foreplay as soon as possible. His own physical pleasure, concentrated almost entirely in his copulatory organ, drives him toward coitus as the goal. For better communication in Phase Five, he should await her signals. An enticing tug or inviting shift in position will show when she's ready. Before her go sign, coitus is premature.

For both sexes, an effective touch zone in foreplay is the chest area, which is supplied by branches of sensitive *intercostal nerves*. Replete with free nerve endings and sensual receptors called *Meissner's corpuscles* and *Merkel's disks*, nipples are supersensitive to light touch. The clitoris, penis, forehead, soles of the feet, palms of the hands, and pads of the fingertips all contain dense concentrations of these specialized nerve endings, making them rich targets in foreplay.

As erogenous zones, breasts significantly vary. Some women feel nothing at all sexual when their breasts are touched, while others orgasm when a nipple or its areolar skin is softly stimulated. Many women and many men identify the nipple as their chest's most erotic area. Studies find that larger breasts feel less nipple or skin sensations than smaller ones (Berman and Berman, 2001). In both genders, a caress to the temple, forehead, or cheeks may cause visible stiffening of the nipples. An erect nipple can show you've sent the right cues.

A neglected erogenous zone is the saddle area of your partner's *perineum* or "sexual skin," a hairless area between the genital organs and anus. As primates, our sexual skin is filled with free nerve endings,

Meissner's corpuscles, and Merkel's disks, making it a source of arousal in many men and some women (Berman and Berman, 2001). Because a woman is more variable in Phase Five, as a man you should watch for "comfort level" cues—such as muscle relaxation, a positive signal, or pulling away, a negative sign—to tell how far to go.

Additional touch zones in foreplay are the outer and inner thighs and the curvilinear buttocks. The word *buttock* derives from the seven-thousand-year-old Indo-European root, *bhau-*, which means "to strike." A touch to the backside stimulates the *pudendal* nerve, which activates the penis and clitoris directly. In tandem with the pudendal nerve, gluteal and perineal branches of the *posterior femoral cutaneous* nerve may be strummed in preparation for coitus. These nerves are plentiful in the inner thighs, backs of the legs, and derrière.

Light touches to these areas travel an evolutionary-old nerve pathway, the *anterior spinothalamic tract*, to pleasure centers where the sensations are enjoyed. Caressed with the right touch cues—a kiss, a nuzzle, light massage—your partner's body shifts into the relaxed parasympathetic mode, "rest-and-digest," which is required for sexual tissues to lubricate and enlarge. Slow sweeping motions of the palms and fingertips across the shoulders, back, and hips can be soothing and arousing at the same time. A parasympathetic response counteracts the sympathetic "fight-or-flight" symptoms felt earlier when you were not yet acquainted. Cold hands become warmer and gastrointestinal muscles relax. Emotionally "all is well."

Compared to a woman, a man's sexual anatomy is simple, standardized, and straightforward: his penis. Despite advice by women's magazines on exotic ways to "Turn Him On Tonight," there is really no mystery because this sexual organ is easily stimulated and quickly satisfied. Nor, at five or more inches when inflated, is it easily missed.

In contrast, a woman's sexual terrain is partially hidden, discretely distributed, and semisubterranean. It is less standardized, more complex, incredibly more mysterious. Without a mental map, men lose their way.

Courtship fails to thrive on misunderstandings, miscues, and deceptive orgasms. Should he fail to communicate with her body, she should educate him in words or take his hand and guide him. The longevity of a relationship depends on verbal and nonverbal honesty.

In his book, *Emotional Intelligence* (1995), Daniel Goleman suggests that the physical closeness, shared desire, aligned intentions, and synchronous body movements of lovemaking lead couples to the same deep feelings of empathy enjoyed by mothers and infants.

The Love Bond

After making love, couples may verbally vow to love forever. Through body language, lovers give and receive more bonding cues than at any other stage of courtship. So many messages go back and forth that they feel closer than either surmised. The chemical cue oxytocin plays a role.

Thanks to the release of oxytocin, couples tend to be faithful to each other, have less desire for others, and feel cheated should the partner be unfaithful. Nonverbal signals reinforce the newly formed bond's exclusiveness. Full-body contact imprints a tactile image of warmth that sticks in memory after lovemaking. The skin's musky aromas register in emotion centers of the mammalian brain. The physical posture itself—usually face-to-face, eye-to-eye, bosom-to-bosom—helps couples psychologically fuse.

From foreplay to coitus, a third type of sexual communication takes place in the Lovemaking Phase. Biologists call it the *postcopulatory display*. Many animals separate after mating, but some intensify the pair bond with additional signs. Zebras groom each other after sex. Antelope lick their mates to release oxytocin. Male avocets (long-legged shore birds) keep one wing stretched over a female's back as they run forward with their bills crossed.

We, too, exchange "après sex" messages. Though previously unidentified, postcopulatory displays may be as important for humans as what comes before or during intercourse itself. To study après-sex communication, we searched personal diaries on the Internet. A search on the phrase "after we made love" revealed clearly readable après-sex behaviors that signaled either "Stay with me" or "Go away."

"After We Made Love"—Positive and Negative Signs

STAY WITH ME. *After we made love* for the first time, we held each other and cried. *After we made love* I tipped my head to hers, a position we call the "meeting of our minds." *After we made love*, we would lie next to each other, bodies touching, holding hands, and sipping wine, and then go to sleep. About half an hour *after we made love*, a chilling breeze blew, and he held me in his arms. It was the full-body massages *after we made love* that made the difference between just having sex and making love. *After we made love*, he said, "We fit like a glove." *After we made love*, my new boyfriend admired my legs. Before we married, she would put on my yellow sneakers *after we made love* in the afternoon. I asked if I could run a brush through her hair *after we made love*. A kiss to my forehead *after we made love*, was the sweetest thing you could have done. *After we made love*, we'd go out barefoot onto the back steps. First time *after we made love* he turned me on my side and snuggled in behind me. The perfect kiss happened *after we made love*, when you took my hand and placed it in yours.

GO AWAY. Comedian Joan Rivers joked that after making love, her husband drew an outline around her body with a piece of chalk. *After we* *made love*, you turned away, only thinking of yourself. You should never have pushed me away *after we made love*. She asked me to leave the bedroom *after we made love*. Lying in bed at night *after we made love*, he stroked the off-white fur of the caribou that hung over his bed. *After we made love*, she threw up. Then she started leaving our bed *after we made love*. After we made love in the afternoon, he seemed restless. *After we made love*, she had told me she was going to New York. "I'm married," I told her *after we made love*. *After we made love*, he said, "I don't think this is going anywhere." *After we made love*, he said, "I got to get up early" and he left. He hated when I went straight to the shower *after we made love*, to wash him off. You really should have talked to me *after we made love*.

What begins with an attention-attracting cue—"I am here"—concludes with a feeling: "We are one." Where one alone stood, two stand now. This is not the end of courtship but the beginning of a process designed to keep you emotionally together and physically close. In Chapter 12, we'll explore nonverbal communication for the long-lasting relationship. Meanwhile, let's explore your most attractive bodily feature, your face.

7. THE FACE OF
ATTRACTION

All action is of the mind and the mirror of the
mind is the face, its index the eyes.
—CICERO (106 B.C.–43 B.C.)

YOUR MOST ATTRACTIVE bodily feature is the surface at the
front of your head, from your forehead to your chin, called
the face. To attract a mate, you enhance the visual appeal of
your facial features, skin, and teeth for a more inviting look. The chin,
lips, cheeks, cheekbones, nose, brow line, eye orbits, and hollows of
the temples visually protrude or recede, and you heighten their messages with facial expressions, hairdos, and makeup.

To say "I am female," a woman accents the sinuous curves of her
mouth with lipstick. To say "I am male," a man trims his sideburns to
create blocky, angular shapes at the sides of his face that resemble the
squared-off "sideburn" markings of the male goldfinch. In courtship,
the face is a canvas, tableau, and signboard rolled into one.

To interest others, you put your best face forward. You feature its
good, and mask its less appealing, facets to create a sexually attractive
façade. As an example, the widespread custom of highlighting a
woman's eyes, cheekbones, and lips with makeup also works to downsize her chin. In all corners of the world, a petite chin is considered an
attractive feminine trait. Anthropologist Donald Symons has sug-
gested that a thin, pointed jaw and small lower face signify higher lev-

els of the hormone estrogen. In every society the message of a heart-shaped face is the same: "I am female" (Symons, 1979).

The female forehead is visibly smoother, rounder, and more vertically upright than a man's. His forehead, in turn, displays a more projecting brow ridge (often with a bony prominence above the nose), is not as rounded, and slopes backward more than hers. A woman's lips are smaller but noticeably fuller than a man's, and her lower jaw is smaller in relation to the height of her skull.

R esearch shows that beards neither raise nor lower a man's physical attractiveness.

To intensify his masculine presence, a man with a small chin may wear a beard to make his lower jaw look bigger. Women respond to the face value of the display without question, much as they accept a friend's pencil-thin eyebrows as "real." In matters of facial appearance, primate eyes trust what they see and don't bother to ask why. Like a male orangutan's flaring cheek flanges—designed for no other purpose than to show a bigger face—what visually exists is all that matters. For men with larger chins, the best-face-forward can be either clean shaven or bearded. Research shows that beards do not either raise or lower a man's physical attractiveness.

WHAT'S IN A FACE?

Emotionally, the face is your most expressive body part. It includes twenty-eight surface landmarks, all of which communicate in courtship:

1. skin	5. forehead
2. ears	6. temples
3. earlobes	7. eyes
4. eyebrows	8. upper eyelids

9. lower eyelids
10. eyelashes
11. nose
12. nostrils
13. nostril bulbs
14. cheekbones
15. cheeks
16. philtrum (vertical groove in upper lip)
17. lower lip
18. upper lip
19. jowls
20. facial hair
21. wrinkles
22. moles ("beauty spots")
23. eccrine sweat glands
24. sebacious oil glands
25. apocrine scent glands
26. upper jaw (maxilla)
27. lower jaw (mandible, including chin)
28. teeth

Despite the ability to recognize and recall thousands of faces, we are unable to describe them adequately in words. Identity clues used by the Chicago Police, for instance, consist only of generic words and phrases:

- high, low, wide, or narrow forehead
- smooth, creased, or wrinkled skin
- long, wide, flat, pug, or Roman nose
- wide, narrow, or flared nostrils
- sunken, filled-out, dried, oily, or wrinkled cheeks
- prominent, high, low, wide, or fleshy cheekbones
- mouth corners turned up, down, or level
- thin, medium, or full upper and lower lips (the two may differ in thickness)
- round, oval, pointed, square, or small chin
- double chin, protruding Adam's apple, hanging jowls

Facial movements and the subtle proportions among facial features are harder still to describe. Overall, the human face has become more babylike, less intimidating, and friendlier in its evolution through time. The wider jaw and broader dental arch of our two-million-year-old human ancestor *Homo habilis* belonged to a fearsome-looking face with great biting power. Today, our lower face's smaller, thinner, and weaker features crouch beneath a bulbous forehead that is essentially infantile in appearance. To human eyes, the forehead's helplessness equates with child care, youth, and innocence.

In courtship, the face draws eyes not only with features but with movements. A face need not be stellar to attract a mate. Every face has its own facets, proportions, and visual appeal. Over hundreds of thousands of years—through a process biologists call *sexual selection*—human evolution has generally favored feminine and masculine good looks. After all, our ancestors were comely enough to have attracted mates themselves. More than any of our animal relatives, we rely strongly on facial signs, signals, and cues in courtship. A smile, expressive eyebrows, and a beckoning glance are indispensable.

CLASSIC COURTING FACES

Studies of facial attractiveness show that the most memorable faces are either very ugly or very beautiful. To be good looking, international film stars highlight cheekbones and showcase wide-set eyes, full lips, and unblemished skin. Picture the broad-beamed eyes of Madonna or the boyish good looks of Tom Cruise.

What makes classic faces remarkable are the idiosyncratic "signature" traits that speak in concert with beauty. Tom Cruise's smile and Madonna's Roman nose come to mind. Decades earlier, Hollywood icon Greta Garbo's face was renowned for its near perfect symmetry. James Dean's thick lower lip gave a pouty, androgynous look to the actor's face. When she smiled, Marilyn Monroe's droopy lids defined a seductive pose with "bedroom eyes." When he smiled, Elvis Presley's asymmetrically curled upper lip snarled a "bad-boy" look. When she turned her face in camera lights, Sophia Loren's sizable nose cast shadows on her cheekbones. Today, the idiosyncracies of these famous faces are as memorable as their classic good looks.

How a Face Attracts the Eye

Though the face makes up less than 5 percent of the body's surface area, it is a major carrier of personality, image, and allure. Begun in the mid-1960s, scientific studies of physical attractiveness have confirmed that the face is the body's prime attractor (Patzer, 1985). With its crush of features, no part of our anatomy transmits as many attractive messages as the facial plain. Nor does any bodily surface have more sensory terminals—eyes, nose, lips, ears, tongue, and skin—with which to receive incoming cues. Unique in the animal kingdom, our courtship literally comes to a head in the face.

Anthropologists have learned that, in every society, the ideal courting face begins with the lean jaw line of a young adult, sixteen to twenty years old. The skin is smooth, moist, unlined, and blemish free. The teeth are evenly spaced, and neither project outward nor curve inward. Jaws align without telling overbites or underbites. Chins are neither too short nor too long. The nose is not large enough to upstage other features. Around the globe, attractive faces tend to be symmetrical and balanced, with the left side mirroring the right.

In men, female beauty activates the same pleasure centers of the brain as those activated by chocolate, Cabernet, and cocaine.

Research shows that facial attractiveness declines significantly between the ages of fifteen and thirty-five (Korthase and Trenholme, 1982), but beauty can be maintained for longer periods if you understand how its features appeal. In the 1930s, biologists isolated explicit traits in the resting face that are favored by human beings everywhere. A set of youthful features and proportions—wide-set eyes and full lips set upon smooth, unblemished skin—is thought to be universally attractive in both the male and female face. Across cultures, higher cheekbones, larger eyes, and a shorter distance between the mouth and chin are preferred qualities in women's and men's faces alike (Perrett, May, and Yoshikawa, 1994).

The essential beauty formula is known as the *infantile schema*. In 1939, the template was identified in mammals (including Homo sapiens) by biologist Konrad Lorenz. Lorenz discovered that we are attracted by features of the "baby face." A baby's domed forehead, wide eyes, petite nose, perfect skin, and small lower jaw conspire to make us feel like cuddling and caring. We are smitten with what biologists call the *cute response*. As we age, the face takes on adult characteristics—wider cheekbones, bigger brow ridges, and larger jaws—but the baby face continues to appeal throughout life.

Precisely these youthful traits are what women and increasing numbers of men strive to preserve through makeup, face cream, cosmetic surgery, and Botox. Wrinkles or blemishes that compete with the infantile schema can be disguised, hidden, and actually erased. Noses can be de-accented with liquid foundation, eyes can be highlighted with eyeliner, and lips can be pearlized to mimic the pouty, full-lipped look of a baby. (A baby's endearing pucker comes from lip muscles that are developed at the midline for sucking.) In short, essentials of the infantile schema can be prolonged almost indefinitely.

Rated most attractive by women are a man's eyes. His eyes evoke the same maternal-caring response that infant eyes evoke in the *en face* gaze. Because women alert to eyes, a man should regularly trim his eyebrows so they don't compete for attention. Men over thirty-five can take a lesson from TV news anchors. On screen, a touch of makeup under the eyes covers distracting wrinkles and keeps the face from looking devitalized, tired, or "sad." A tiny amount is enough to hide creases without anyone seeing the cover-up. Again, primate eyes trust what they see.

Across cultures, higher cheekbones, larger eyes, and a shorter distance between the mouth and chin are preferred qualities in women's and men's faces.

Research shows that average-looking faces that would not land starring roles or win a beauty contest are still judged moderately to highly attractive. In a classic study, University of Texas psychologists Judith Langlois and Lori Roggman digitally blended men's and women's faces to create a composite "average-looking" male and female face. Judges rated the computer-averaged visages more attractive than any of the real faces used in the composites (Langlois and Roggman, 1990).

Follow-up studies in England and Japan confirmed that average-looking faces are indeed as attractive, if not always as "beautiful," as the actual faces used in the blends (Perrett, May, and Yoshikawa, 1994). Even plain faces without chiseled jaws, sculpted cheekbones, long eyelashes, and other classic beauty traits appeal in courtship. Through the magic of Lorenz's infantile schema, average-looking faces have better than average sex appeal.

Does Your Face Say What You Mean?

If an average face is more attractive than you think, it becomes more appealing still with its features set in motion. Facial movements are as becoming as facial features themselves. Expressive lip, eyelid, and brow motions light up and energize plain-looking faces just as they animate pretty ones. Research in social psychology shows that men judge expressive faces "more attractive" than beautiful ones.

You can head-cock, tilt your face left or right to show empathy, head-toss, clear bangs with a head shake to bring notice to your eyes, lift eyebrows higher to register understanding, and prolong a smile for lingering radiance. A mobile face shows responsiveness, emotes immediacy, and is more entertaining to behold. Since we are primates with highly evolved temporal-lobe modules for facial recognition, a face and its features compel attention like no other body parts.

We pay incredibly close attention to lips. PET-scan studies show that, while listening, we unconsciously read lips to enhance vocal recognition of the words. Lip movements alone, without speech sounds, light up *Wernicke's area*, the brain's primary speech-comprehension center. Since we watch lips closely, they should be well-groomed in courtship. The most beautiful eyes will not divert attention from unsightly, lipstick-smeared, or chapped lips.

Medical EMG or *electromyography* studies disclose measurably higher levels of muscle activity in a woman's face than in a man's. This shows in her eyebrows, for instance, which are more emotional—and more readable—than his. A one-eighth- to one-fifth-second "micro-momentary" downward movement can signal momentary disagreement, sadness, or doubt. The *corrugator* muscles, which contract to pinch and lower the brows above the nasal bridge, show significantly higher EMG responsiveness in women (Manstead, 1998).

Men show higher EMG levels in *masseter muscles*. These are the muscles that close the jaws in biting and involuntarily contract them in anger. Momentary tightening of masseters—which show as knotty bumps in the cheeks below the sideburns—may signal hidden disagreement, displeasure, or dislike.

> Studies show that men are more likely than women to display anger in a conversation.

The chin is highly readable in both sexes. EMG measurements reveal high activity levels in the chin's *mentalis* muscle. As this emotional muscle contracts, small, pitted dimples form on the skin's surface. Feelings that escape notice elsewhere on the body show clearly on the front of the chin.

For unknown reasons, the chin is emotionally responsive in courtship. A quivering chin is the first sign that a partner feels betrayed, hurt, or sad—or that a cry is coming on.

Above the chin is a powerful courtship cue, the smile. In a true or *zygomatic smile*, the mouth corners curve upward and the outer corners of the eyes crinkle into crow's-feet. Though we are taught to show a *polite grin*, the heartfelt smile is hard for anyone but a method actor to perform on command. The polite grin, on the other hand, is easily willed into existence by conscious areas of cerebral cortex. Since it can be manipulated, it is subject to deception. The true smile is mediated by the cingulate gyrus, a part of the brain over which we have little conscious control. Our emotional cingulate generates the sincere smile that reflects how we genuinely feel (Damasio, 1994).

For success in courtship, learn to tell a true smile from its manipulative look-alike, the polite grin. Misreading the grin as a sign of affection can be disheartening when a partner—who has politely smiled at you all afternoon—declines your invitation for a date. In the true smile, lip corners curl *upward* through contraction of zygomaticus muscles. Telltale crow's-feet lines show as the zygomaticus contracts in concert with *orbicularis oculi* muscles around the eyes. In the intentionally polite, social, or sometimes "false" smile, lip corners stretch *sideward* through contraction of less emotional *risorius* muscles. When you see neither upwardly curled lips nor crinkled eyes, your partner may not be ready for dinner and a movie.

Eyebrow Enticements

Specialized edge receptors in the primate brain alert human eyes to borders, frames, and crosscutting lines. Since they indelibly mark the forehead with lines above the eyes, eyebrows play a featured role in courtship. Recall the eyebrow flash of recognition, a universally friendly sign in which brows lift to meet and greet. Biologists have learned that the eyebrow flash is also a worldwide flirtation cue that says, "You appeal to me." To greet a nice-looking partner, we unwittingly contract the forehead's *occipito frontalis* muscles to raise both brows. This muscle group is incredibly emotional because it is controlled by special visceral nerves.

From a study of 255 brow raises in three cultures, behavioral biologists found that people typically elevate when they say "yes" (Grammer et al., 1988). Accompanied by a smile, lifted brows add positive punctuation in courtship by communicating affirmation, interest, empathy, and understanding. They also boost the energy of a smile. This is why women pencil, pluck, and feather their eyebrows, lifting them higher above the natural brow line to create the illusion of a friendlier face.

Glasses Frame Your Face

Like eyebrows, eyeglasses are eye-catching in courtship. Since they stand out, you should be choosy about the frames you wear. Though studies find that eyeglasses do have a "negative or detrimental effect" on facial attractiveness (Patzer, 1985), a strategically chosen design can actually enhance the features of your face.

To line-sensitive primate eyes, frames are as conspicuous as the eyes they enclose. Encircling borders compete for attention, intensify gaze, and give eye contact a piercing quality. Since glasses make eyes seem to stare, periodically remove your spectacles for a softer image.

If your face is very round, balance its circular shape with geometrically squarer frames. Round frames would only accentuate the roundness and give your face an unflattering pie shape. Conversely, square faces look better in round frames that soften angular lines.

Reduce a plump face with frames that are visibly wider than the facial border, measured at the temples. Widen a narrow or rectangular face with frames that don't extend beyond the temples. Downsize a wide forehead with triangular frames that aim upward. Lift droopy eyes with frames that arch upward and outward at the sides. Subtle details of line and angle create illusions that seem "real" to vision centers of the primate brain.

Glasses should not interfere with emotional cues emitted by your eyes, eyelashes, and eyebrows. The upper contour of your frames should follow the curvature of brows without masking flashes of happiness, recognition, and empathy that show as they lift. Neither should glasses hide cheekbones, which are universally attractive in courtship, nor rest too heavily on your cheeks to create a "tired" look. With the right frames, your face is brought into balance.

Beauty Marks

Growing evidence suggests that facial symmetry is universally attractive in courtship. Yet complete balance is not always best. Asymmetries on the facial plain can attract favorable attention and enhance beauty.

A case in point is supermodel Cindy Crawford. Her face has graced more magazine covers than anyone else's in history. Crawford's face is symmetrical, though her left eye opens slightly wider, and her left eyebrow rides a bit higher than its counterpart on the right. Her asymmetrical case in point is literally a point, a tiny mole above the corner of her left lip.

You may wonder what an imperfection adds to beauty. For Cindy Crawford the dark dot draws attention as an exception to the bilateral symmetry of her face. Psychologically, it shows she is less than perfect, less divine, more human, and thus more accessible. Subliminally, the defect grants permission to approach.

In the West, facial moles are called "beauty marks." European women once wore a small black dot on the cheek as a fashion statement. In motion pictures, beauty marks have played starring roles on faces since the earliest films were made. Beauty marks of such Hollywood stars as Marilyn Monroe, Elizabeth Taylor, and Lisa Minnelli attract eyes to their faces, while the marks themselves go unnoticed. Today some women undergo *dermapigmentation* and tattoo a mole-size mark on the cheek to invite eyes. The appealing message, "Notice me," makes it harder for men to glance away.

When Eyes Meet

Five hundred million years in the making, horizontally paired eyes are the main focus of faces today. Eyes accent the horizontal aspects of a human face by counteracting the strong verticality of its freestanding nose. Meeting someone for the first time, we almost always orient to eyes.

Social psychologist Arthur Aron has studied the power of eye contact in relationships. After a ninety-minute conversation in which total strangers shared personal details about themselves and their feelings, subjects were asked to gaze silently into each other's eyes for a period of four minutes. Many reported strong feelings of attraction afterward, and some couples eventually married. What Aron studied experimentally happens naturally in courtship's Conversation Phase. You spend hours negotiating the rules of visual engagement to achieve what his subjects accomplished in four minutes: a perceptible feeling of love.

In its relaxed, resting position, the lower lid of your partner's open eye barely touches the bottom circumference of the iris. The upper eyelid covers a good deal of its top. Excited by your presence, eyes open wider, and more of each iris shows. Strongly attracted, your partner's top eyelids may slightly droop. Drooping, bedroom eyes show that the rest-and-digest response has engaged and that your partner's visceral brain is in a receptive mood.

By six weeks of age, babies smile at black geometric spots, perceiving them as "eyes."

The most powerful eye contact is "love at first sight." Called "the thunderbolt" in French (*le coup de foudre*) and "the arrow's strike" in Spanish (*el flechazo*), love at first sight establishes a visual link like the *en face* gaze that binds mother and child. When adult eyes meet, they ordinarily repel like colliding billiard balls. In love at first sight, eye contact is prolonged. Lengthy mutual gaze shows when two people are simultaneously smitten. Should couples lock eyes for longer than the usual one- or two-second glance, lightning may indeed strike.

There are no controlled studies of love at first sight. Nevertheless, many couples report having the experience. Available evidence shows that men are more easily smitten than women (Canary and Emmers-Sommer, 1997). In men, eye contact with a pretty face activates the *ventral striatum*, a reptilian pleasure center that perhaps plays a role in love at first sight. In a survey of 1,495 adults, two-thirds (64 percent) believed that falling in love within an hour of first seeing someone is a real possibility. Of the poll's 958 believers, more than half (58 percent) had experienced love at first sight themselves. Of these, half (55 percent) married the partner, and three-quarters (76 percent) of them are still married (Naumann, 2001).

Men are more easily affected than women by love at first sight.

A CASE OF LOVE AT FIRST SIGHT

It is called love at first sight for a reason. Justin saw Caitlin from his car window and was "instantly attracted." Caitlin was on her front porch waiting for him to arrive. Friends had arranged a blind date, a drive to the Puyallup Fair near Seattle. Before they met, Justin had

CONTINUED ON NEXT PAGE

never heard the sound of Caitlin's voice, never felt the touch of her hand, never smelled her perfume. It was the sight of her standing there, calmly meeting his gaze, that made him ache to be near her.

The feeling was not sexual or below the belt, he recalled, but a powerful longing to be physically close. "It was like the universe shifted," he said, "and we were always going to be together." They had trouble speaking at first but walked and talked at the fair as if they were longtime friends. She hand-fed him a bite of her hamburger, and after a long-distance courtship (Justin lived in San Diego), they married.

Caitlin had been visually infatuated as well. Before touching his shoulder or hearing him speak, she liked how he held her gaze. She noticed that his eyes crinkled obliquely at the sides. "I've always liked those kinds of eyes," she said.

Love at first sight is just that, a physiological reaction in which eye contact triggers specific changes in the brain. The pull of physical attraction comes with the draw of parental attachment, the latter not rooted in sexuality but in the mother-infant bond. You feel attracted to the person you see, and emotionally attached at the same time. According to Rutgers anthropologist Helen Fisher, love at first sight evolved as a primitive and powerful part of romance that is seen in cultures around the world today.

What are the brain circuits for falling in love? Neuropsychologist Semir Zeki at London's University College imaged the brains of men and women who had recently fallen in love. As subjects viewed photographs of their dearly beloved, Zeki found heightened activity in the forebrain's anterior cingulate cortex, which is associated with feelings of happiness and euphoria, in the *medial insula*, also involved with emotion, and in two regions of the basal ganglia, the *putamen* and *caudate nucleus*.

These are the likely brain areas aroused by love at first sight. So powerful is the thunderbolt that it sweeps couples off their feet and hurls them headlong into love before they have a chance to wink, shake hands, or say hello.

Hidden Meaning in Hair

Human beings spend an incredible amount of time noticing and commenting on one another's hair. In part, this is because we are mammals for whom carefully groomed hair betokens high status, good health, and cleanliness. The biological equivalent of scales, feathers, and fur, hair not only keeps our head warm and dry but also protects the braincase from heat, cold, and sunshine. Hair once provided camouflage to help our ancestors blend into the natural landscape. Today's hairstyles help us blend into the social landscape as well.

Hair gives the face a perceptual border. Consider a portrait with the top of its frame missing. The image seems unbalanced, because your brain's visual centers perceive the contents as being less tied together than when cognitively linked inside the frame. This explains why some men dislike the bald look, not just because hair loss is a sign of aging but because balding makes the facial features seem unframed. Without a top border, eyes look smaller in proportion to the forehead. Unframed, the landscape looms larger, and eyes shrink proportionally to the gestalt.

The males of our species have been using potions for baldness since Egyptian times three thousand years ago. In 400 B.C., Hippocrates concocted a remedy of opium, spices, horseradish, and pigeon droppings to cure the affliction, but the Father of Medicine remained bald. And yet, in courtship, baldness gives the head an infant appeal which, by virtue of the innocence it connotes, makes a hairless man easier to approach. The tactile appeal of exposed, shiny skin on such a rounded surface evokes a desire to reach out and touch the friendly pate.

From cross-cultural studies, anthropologists have learned that shaved heads and short hair in men symbolize discipline, denial, and conformity (Alford, 1996). Longer hair shows openness, passion, and lack of inhibition. Mimicking thorns, barbs, and spines, spiked hair seems a little daring and dangerous: "Do not touch." The style a woman prefers reflects her personality as well as his.

> In women, long hair signifies uninhibited, passionate emotion. Masculine long hair projects all brawn and no brains, carelessness, and a good-natured personality.

A woman's hair is more aesthetically expressive than a man's. Skillfully cut bangs cover and "shrink" the forehead, proportionally increasing the size, appeal, and presence of feminine eyes. The softness and touchable nature of tresses invites handling. Curly hair especially, according to New York hairstylist and author of *Curly Girl* Lorraine Massey, is tactile, flirty, and playful (Massey, 2002). The provocative message of curly hair is "Touch me."

Young women with unlined foreheads may wear their hair pulled back off the top and sides of the face. As age brings horizontal wrinkles and vertical frown lines, hair may be worn with bangs. For many, wispy short or whimsically longer bangs define an attractive frame for the brows and eyes. Bangs showcase the lips and cheekbones, downsize the nose, and mask creases that detract from the infantile schema.

Hairstyle plays a prominent role in first impressions. Ethnographic research shows that long hair in women signifies uninhibited, passionate emotion (Alford, 1996). A study by Yale psychologist Marianne LaFrance finds that women's short, tousled hair conveys confidence and an outgoing personality but ranks low in sexuality. Medium-length casual hair suggests intelligence and "good nature," whereas long, straight, blond hair projects sexuality and affluence. For men, LaFrance says, medium-length, side-parted hair connotes intelligence, affluence, and a "narrow mind" in first impressions. Masculine long hair projects all brawn and no brains, carelessness, and a good-natured personality. A man's short, front-flip hairstyle, with the bangs combed stiffly upward, is perceived as confident, sexy, and self-centered. In the masculine front flip, bangs ascend in a topknot, not unlike the tuft of a displaying male bird.

In courtship, a man's hairstyle attracts notice like the crest, comb, tuft, or topknot of a displaying male bird.

The full or close-cropped look of our head's furry mane explains traditional contrasts between men's and women's hair. Short, military cuts show off masculine power traits: bony brow ridges, prominent noses, and larger jaws. Longer, thicker hair showcases feminine eyes and lips while downplaying noses, jaws, and chins. Men project added strength with beards that widen the lower face and with mustaches that turn the lip corners downward, projecting a "fierce" face only a smile can soften.

Lead with Your Face

Faces attract through eyes, cheekbones, and features of the baby face. In courtship an average-looking face has the same leverage as a beautiful face, sometimes even more. Fashion-model beauty is often intimidating, and some people shy away. Ironically, a face that is too good-looking may be unapproachable.

A n average-looking face has the same leverage as a beautiful face. and sometimes more.

Your face is your most attractive bodily feature. Constituting only 5 percent of your bodily surface, it carries 95 percent of your allure. The character your face reflects is your leading edge in courtship. In the next chapter, we explore what lies beneath the facial plain—the body itself. If your face shows who you are in courtship, your body suggests what you do.

8. HOW BODIES ATTRACT

I have always tried to render inner feelings
through the mobility of the muscles. . . .
—AUGUSTE RODIN

T HE HUMAN BODY comes in two basic designs: male and female. Over a century ago, Charles Darwin described the female body as being essentially "rounder" than that of a man.
A woman has a thicker insulating layer of adipose tissue beneath the
skin, which makes her body pleasingly softer to touch. Visually, the
fatty layer smooths out muscular bulges, bony bumps, and tendons to
create a feminine form of more fluid lines. Local deposits of fat on
her upper arms, neck, and shoulders over the trapezius muscles;
breasts; hips over the pelvic girdle's contoured crests; pubic area form-
ing the fleshy mount of Venus; buttocks; and outer thighs define a
shape men have admired since our species began two hundred thousand years ago.

The Venus Shape

Two millennia ago, defining traits of female attractiveness were celebrated in statues of Venus, the Roman goddess of physical beauty and
sexual love. Many today regard her likenesses, like that of the now-
armless *Venus de Milo*, as models of perfection in feminine grace. The

ancient statues exhibit smooth bodies, gracile necks, rounded breasts, sinuous shoulders, full hips, and narrow waists.

The narrow waist of Venus, you should note, is not as slender as the sveltely constricted waist of a *Vogue* model. In all likelihood, the classic Venus form would not win a Miss Universe contest. Yet the shape that has survived for two thousand years as an artistic beauty standard continues to work remarkably well in courtship today. A woman need not display the super-thin waist of a supermodel to attract attention. Her body achieves full potency with the natural, and classically more beguiling, sex-goddess shape of a Venus.

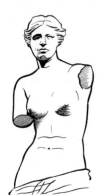

Venus de Milo illustrates the ideal shape of a woman.

A woman need not display the super-thin waist of a super-model to attract attention.

The David Shape

Darwin described the males of our species as being taller, heavier, and stronger than the females and as having "squarer shoulders and more plainly-pronounced muscles" (Darwin, 1871:867). Artistically, Michelangelo's *David* statue has long exemplified the muscular body beautiful for men. Michelangelo carved optimal masculine traits in stone five hundred years ago, and little has changed since.

Looking at the statue, the first thing you notice is David's sinewy right wrist and hand curled onto his right thigh. Male hands are esteemed by women because they signify energy, strength, and masculine protectiveness. Michelangelo suggests David's willingness to protect and serve by exaggerating the size and showcasing the placement of his right hand.

Next you see David's right biceps muscle, which is definitely virile but not oversized as in the swollen arms of a bodybuilder. His wide shoulders, narrow waist, and essential wedge shape suggest strength without the intimidation of a larger Hercules, Atlas, or Incredible Hulk frame. David's abdominal muscles show the softer definition women prefer to the harder washboard abs featured in men's magazines. Proportionally, David's is the quintessential masculine shape, lean and strong—yet neither too lean nor too strong for comfort.

Michelangelo's *David* represents the ideal male body. (Note his contrapposto stance.)

The Right Stance

As attractive as the physical shapes of Venus and David are, their *contrapposto* stance makes them more appealing still. The marble figures

pose in counterbalanced "action" postures that signal inner motivation and psychological response. Their bodies seem to twist from
head to legs to feet, even as they stand in place. That the planes of
their shoulders and hips—as well as those of their knees and feet—
are held in coordinated opposition makes Venus and David more
lively to behold. The asymmetrical arrangement of body parts catches
your attention and teases your fancy.

Placing a human's body weight fully on the right foot in a contrapposto stance causes the right hip to raise and protrude, and the right
shoulder to dip. On the body's left side, the hip lowers while the shoulder lifts. With its antithetical blend of limb extension, flexion, and tor-
sion, an otherwise frozen statue comes alive with movement and feeling.

Appealing for attention through body language, the contrapposto
stance is as powerful in courtship as it is in art. The animated posture
gives a partner the impression that you are, by the way you hold your
body, more engaged, more connected, and more attentive. In short,
you project a greater degree of nonverbal *immediacy*. Defined by psychologist Albert Mehrabian, "postural immediacy" communicates
greater directness, intensity, and feeling to those with whom you inter-
act (Mehrabian, 1967).

Even without her arms, the second century B.C. *Venus de Milo* is
charming and engagingly full of life. Carrying her body weight on the
right foot, Venus turns her head slightly left above her raised left
shoulder. At the same time, bending her left leg as if to step forward,
she twists the limb suggestively rightward to bring attention to her
knee. Venus's right hip raises and protrudes, accenting the curvature
of her waist.

As a nonverbal statement, Venus's contrapposto stance is more engaging than the static "wooden" pose of ancient Egyptian statues,
which seem unnaturally frozen and devoid of feeling. The stiffer
Egyptian stance—with level shoulders, level hips, and both feet

planted firmly on the ground—resembles the immobile "shy" postures some adopt in courtship. Anxiety shows as they stand rigidly in place without moving.

As for David, his contrapposto stance is seemingly balanced between thought and action, between relaxation and coiled strength. Michelangelo positioned David to stand with his body weight squarely on the right foot, with his left rotating freely away. In his energetic yet relaxed pose, David seems poised to step left as if moving in that direction. He carries his left hip lower than his right because, like a pitcher before the windup, David's body is positioned to sling a stone at Goliath. The asymmetrical stance—in which his straightened and weight-bearing right leg opposes his slightly bent and resting left—is an intention cue showing David is about to approach.

In courtship, a man may use David's stance to show interest in a partner, interest balanced by restraint. The "windup" posture—standing with the weight on one foot while seeming to step ahead with the other—suggests that he wishes to move forward, and yet it shows he's also holding back, keeping his body in check until invited closer. The weight-bearing limb shows restraint, while the stepping limb angles forward as if to approach.

The asymmetry of contrapposto's weight-shift attracts greater notice than a symmetrical stance with the body weight distributed equally on two feet at once. Whereas the former connotes vitality, the latter suggests hesitation and reserve.

For a more vibrant pose, a woman may adopt the lithesome, torso-twisting posture of fashion models by rotating her pelvic and shoulder girdles in opposite directions. The position of her torso will connote a feeling of aliveness and spontaneity through its counterpoised semblance of rotational movement. As sculptor Auguste

Rodin taught, inner feelings show through the mobility of the muscles. Indeed, motion underpins the word *emotion*, which evolved from the ancient Indo-European root *meue-*, for "mobile."

DETAILS DEFINE DIFFERENCES

The bodies of Venus and David differ, though not as clearly or dramatically as those of some animal species. Extravagant sexual traits—bright color patches, huge feather plumes, and spreading antlers brought about through sexual selection—have not evolved in the human body, though we make up for them with eye-catching hats, colorful clothing, and trendy shoes. Our bodies contrast in comparatively minor ways, but even tiny cues are noteworthy in courtship. Considered attractive around the world, subtle differences between a man and a woman are highlighted with distinctive lines, shapes, patterns, and markings:

- A woman's collarbone is horizontally placed, or slopes slightly downward to the sides, to make her neck look longer and slimmer than that of a man. A choker or necklace effectively marks the gender contrast with an eye-catching line.
- A man's collarbone rises laterally, making his neck look shorter and thicker than that of a woman. Like the inflatable ruff of a frilled lizard, a rising shirt collar frames, accents, and "widens" his neck to mark the physical difference in size.
- Unlike a man's, a woman's neck may be encircled by two to four horizontal skin creases, lines of flexure called "rings of Venus." A silk scarf worn below the Adam's apple suggestively echoes her neck's softer, feminine look.
- According to NASA, a woman's hand is 12 percent smaller than a man's. It has a narrow, tapering shape, and the index finger may be longer than the middle digit. Painting her longer nails with colorful polish accentuates the slimness and taper of her hand.
- A man's knee is protruding, angular, and bony. A woman's knee is rounder, plumper, more pleasing to the eye. Her kneecaps are less conspicuous, so the knee looks softer to

the touch. Dresses, skirts, and shorts reveal the roundness for all to see.

- A woman's calf muscles ride lower on the leg than a man's ride on his. A mid-length skirt reveals the subtle contrast, bringing attention to the difference with a swaying hemline.

- Feminine wrists and ankles are thinner than male ones. Women call attention to slim extremities with thin watchbands, delicate bracelets, and dainty straps. Men visibly magnify their own larger wrists and stouter ankles with encircling sleeves and cuffs.

- A woman's foot is 10 percent narrower than a man's. Though not a major difference, it invites major notice. To enhance the illusion of slimness, a woman wears thinner, tapering shoes to drive the contrast home: "I am female."

To a woman, a nice man is physically more attractive than a good-looking man who is not nice.

Anatomy of Sexual Traits

When a child is born the first question asked is, "Boy or girl?" Gender is one of humankind's oldest, deepest, and most vital classifications. Without hesitation, we typecast everyone we meet into an appropriate gender role. In French, Russian, German, and many of the world's languages, even inanimate objects are grammatically masculine or feminine in form. In Spanish, the moon is "female" and the sun is "male."

To determine the sex of a newborn, we look for what biologists call *primary sexual traits*. Penis indicates a boy, and labial folds a girl. In some baby girls we see slightly swollen breasts as well. The latter, a *secondary* sexual trait, may be brought out prematurely by release of the maternal hormone estrogen into the infant's body.

Apart from primary sexual traits, newborns look much alike. Boys and girls start out in the embryonic stage with bodies that are basically female. Except for external genitalia, male and female babies give off basically the same feminine cues. For instance, both sexes display feminine nipples.

In childhood, visible sex differences begin to bloom as the male hormone androgen literally makes a boy from a girl. Similarly, estrogen acts on the female template, pulling the body further along a path to womanhood. And yet, other than from genital organs themselves or from cultural cues evident in clothing and hair length, it may be hard to tell if a ten-year-old child is a boy or a girl.

As puberty arrives, visible gender contrasts appear on the body. Hormones further masculinize or feminize the adolescent form. Secondary sexual traits sprout on trunks and limbs that were childlike months before. Male and female anatomies mature reproductively between the ages of eleven and fifteen, and external cues telegraph the news for everyone to see.

After puberty's cascade of sex-shaping hormones, the bodies of young men and women continue to grow further apart. Males do not become twice the size of females—as they do in our mountain gorilla cousins—but differences are telling nonetheless. Women become noticeably curvy as bodies adapt for childbearing. Breasts enlarge; hips widen. Deposits of fatty tissue accumulate on upper arms, bottoms, and thighs as a food reserve for pregnancy.

Evolution of Sexual Beauty

The female body, like the female face, has several built-in "infant appeals"—babylike features—that attract notice by suggesting immaturity. The baby template, or *kinderschema*, shows in a woman's smaller stature, thinner neck, narrower shoulders, and more nearly hairless skin, as well as in limbs that are smaller in proportion to her torso. Relatively shorter legs, along with the wider carrying angle her upper leg bone assumes with the pelvis, make a woman's gait noticeably different from a man's, with more hip roll and buttock sway. The "wiggle in her walk" is an eye-catching immaturity cue that shows off her legs, thighs, and derrière.

Many men find short women unusually attractive. Smaller stature infantilizes the female body, giving it a cuter, "childlike" look.

On the other side of the gender continuum, evolution has specialized men for running, throwing, hunting, and defending. Just as the male face grows longer, wider, and heavier—essentially "fiercer"—a man's body enlarges to intimidate rivals. Like bigger noses, brow ridges, and jaws, the larger body size, pronounced muscle mass, and thick skeletal frame suggest masculine strength and vigor.

Men are taller and heavier. They have bigger hearts and lungs, more blood hemoglobin, more muscle tissue, and less body fat than women. A man has longer legs and forearms, bigger feet, and thicker hands, all of which made him, in prehistoric times, a more efficient hunter, scavenger, and warrior—and today, a more worthy opponent of his competitors in courtship, fellow men. Females key to his athletic gender signs, as well. A study of thousands of women from diverse cultures by psychologist David Buss confirms that women are universally attracted to men who offer physical protection (Buss, 1998).

For the most part, beauty standards are uniform throughout the world. In every society, the body beautiful starts with the frame of a healthy seventeen- to twenty-two-year-old in whom the full complement of secondary sexual traits is apparent. If you wondered why the bodies of Venus and David are youthful, it's because gender cues show with greater clarity on young-adult frames. Unlike other mammals who rely on smell, we are very visual primates in courtship and are attracted by cues we can see.

A beauty standard that does vary across cultures is body weight. Native Hawaiians, for example, found heavier bodies attractive, while thinner figures are fancied today in the Western world. Yet even body size has rather narrow limits in courtship. In every society, when thinness or obesity interferes with messages emitted by secondary-sexual traits—when midriffs eclipse hips or when curvature gives way to emaciation—attractiveness wanes.

Deciphering Body Parts

We respond to David's wedge shape, Venus's hourglass figure, and the asymmetry of a contrapposto stance through *gestalt laws* of perception. *Gestalt*, the German word for "shape," refers to a coherent pattern, configuration, or organized whole. The statues' component parts are secondary to the whole, and the whole is different from the sum of its parts. Yet as we notice the psychological big picture, we respond to distinctly separate areas of the body—to buttocks, legs, midriffs, feet, and so on—at the same time.

Partialism is the psychiatric term for an exclusive attraction to a specific body part—to the hands, ears, or neck, for instance. For those who have abnormal partialism, such as a foot fetish, the body part alone may stimulate intense sexual feelings and fantasies. For the average person with normal partialism, the favored area is simply more appealing than other body parts. Men may be aroused by the sight of breasts or legs, for example, while women may find shoulders or buttock shape pleasing.

According to biologist Alfred Kinsey, while men appreciate the unclothed female figure, women find frontal nudity repellent in men.

Highlighting the features to which your partner is partial helps you become physically more attractive. Contrary to what men assume, a woman may not relish the sight of overly developed biceps or forearms with prominent veins. On the other hand, men find a woman's muscles generally appealing. Her veins, softened by a layer of adipose tissue, are less likely to show. Unless they themselves are bodybuilders, women are not unduly impressed by a man's washboard abs. A lean abdomen is attractive; muscular lumps are not.

A well-developed *rectus abdominis* muscle and its fibrous bands of connective tissue show a "six-pack" shape when not covered—as they usually are—by fatty tissue in abdominal skin. There is no evidence that women find a washboard look any more appealing than a smoother-looking abdomen. According to psychiatrist Katharine Phillips, coauthor of *The Adonis Complex*, advertising and popular culture have conspired to make men as aware of their muscle definition as women are aware of their figures and weight (Pope, Phillips, and Olivardia, 2000). Today's media images set unrealistic standards for males and females alike.

Growing numbers of teens and young adults suffer from BDD, *body dysmorphic disorder*. BDD is an obsessive preoccupation with one's perceived bodily defects. "I hate my body" is the usual complaint. Shame and humiliation keep some from approaching others thought to be more attractive. Like many psychiatric disorders, there is a continuum in BDD ranging from mild to severe. Many fault their size or shape for not matching ideal types seen in movies or on TV. Young girls in particular compare their bodies to thinner physiques in the media. In a study of 548 adolescent girls from grades five to twelve, seven in ten reported that magazine photos of fashion models influenced their image of bodily perfection. Harvard Medical School researcher Alison Field, the study's director, found that almost half felt a need to lose weight (Field et al., 1999).

Fortunately, the body below the neck plays less of a leading role in courtship than young people think. As Gordon Patzer concluded from an exhaustive summary of research on physical attractiveness, "The role of physique as a component of physical attractiveness is a very distant second to the face" (Patzer, 1985:160). If a perfect body were required, few would court.

According to the *matching hypothesis*, people tend to choose partners whose level of bodily attractiveness approximates their own. Couples who are alike in attractiveness are more likely than mismatched pairs to continue dating.

That we are content with a partner's less-than-perfect body size or shape is explained by the *satisfaction principle*. As soon as we encounter someone who is good enough—who exhibits just a few of our favored features—we feel satisfied. The search for perfection gives way to an appreciation for what we see, and at least momentarily, we stop looking for the optimal body. Instead, we become what psychologists call "satisficers."

According to Herbert Simon, the Nobel Prize–winning economist who coined the term in 1957, a *satisficer* is anyone who would stop searching in a haystack after finding the first needle. The opposite, a *maximizer*, is someone who would keep searching a haystack for the perfect needle. Swarthmore psychologist Barry Schwartz finds that satisficers are generally happier than maximizers with the choices they make. His research suggests that maximizers have more relationship problems because they are always looking for someone better. Over time, evolution produced significantly more satisficers than maximizers. Since they are too picky to find a mate and settle down, maximizers are less likely to bear offspring. In effect, courtship's satisfaction principle has stacked the deck with satisficers who look on your body's bright side.

Neck and Neck

A woman's neck is slimmer and proportionally longer than a man's. The bony superstructure of her shoulder girdle is markedly delicate. A man's thicker neck houses a more angular and prominently bulging Adam's apple. By comparison, the female Adam's apple is smaller and flatter in appearance. Because it reveals a gender difference, both men and women profit when they show rather than cover the neck in courtship.

Shoulder Speak

Shoulders, the paired, jointed girdle connecting arms to the torso, are considered attractive around the world. Their horizontal, angular shape gives the human frame its signature, squared-off silhouette. Rounded deltoid muscles of the upper arms soften the angularity with their curvilinear contour. These conspicuous body parts are singled out for display with shoulder pads that emphasize breadth and with off-the-shoulder blouses and puffy sleeves that feature the deltoids' roundness.

In their book *Instant Style*, Emily Cho and Neila Fisher write: "We think one of the best fashion attributes 'you are born with' is a great pair of shoulders" (Cho and Fisher, 1996:40). They assess your underrated shoulders accurately. Their shapes and suggestive movements attract as much attention as bosoms, buttocks, and waists. Shoulders have as much to say in courtship as they do in fashion, acting, and dance. One shrug, like the proverbial picture, is worth a thousand words.

Though not on top of a man's most-attractive list, shoulders are among a woman's most expressive body parts. Controlled, like the muscles of facial expression, by special visceral nerves, their movements are impulsive, volatile, and seductive. Their roundness and smoothness draw eyes to a female's more delicate collarbone, graceful neck, and softer skin. At night, a woman may bare her shoulders to reflect evening's artificial light. The skin's luminance brings attention to the neck and upper body while brightening her face and eyes.

Since shoulders show strength, women prefer bigger shoulders in men. Studies find that both males and females judge wider shoulders "more attractive" in men than narrow ones (Horvath, 1979). Their size and silhouette when squared define a physically commanding posture called the *broadside display*. Biologically, the impression of strength encoded in shoulders evolved from a vertebrate-wide dominance posture used by fish, reptiles, mammals, and primates. To appear physically powerful, men and other males with backbones display expanded versions of themselves to loom larger than they truly are: A codfish turns the widest part of its body to bluff rivals; frogs puff up fraudulently to seem bigger; chameleons turn a broadside to expand; gorillas beat their chest with cupped hands to show strength.

A woman's shoulders are smaller because her collarbone is shorter, thinner, and horizontally configured. A man's shoulders are bigger because his collarbone is longer, thicker, and rise as they span outward to the sides.

The Outspoken Chest

The female trunk is longer than a male's in relation to total body height. A woman's thorax (between the neck and diaphragm) is shorter, cone-shaped, and graced with breasts. A man's thorax is longer and has vestigial breasts with feminine nipples. In courtship, his bared torso is not as pleasing to the eye as he thinks. Should he bare it, 68 percent of readers recently polled by *Cosmopolitan* prefer a hairless look. Older women surveyed by Cambridge University researchers prefer hairy chests. While the preference for masculine shoulders is constant, fondness for chest hair changes with the times.

Women find moderate torso size in men more physically attractive than larger, barrel chests. Research shows that Charles Atlas–style up-per bodies are generally unattractive (Beck et al., 1976). Overall, women find average-size male torsos more attractive and prefer mus-cular *mesomorphic* to plumper *endomorphic* or skinnier *ectomorphic* builds. Summarizing studies of adult attractiveness, Gordon Patzer writes: "The overwhelmingly favored physique is an average or moderate build. The overwhelmingly disliked physique is the obese or over-weight whereas a mildly unfavorable view exists for the thin or under-weight" (Patzer, 1985:158).

A woman's shallower, less muscled chest displays conspicuous breasts. Breasts enlarge after puberty for no other reason than to send a gender message. In most mammals, mammary glands do not de-velop until near the end of pregnancy. In humans, the growth of adi-pose breast tissue is one the first visible changes in puberty. According to biologist Caroline Pond, the fatty deposits themselves serve no physiological function in nursing (Pond, 1997). Chimps and other pri-mate females have breasts that inflate only when filled with milk. If a mother ape isn't nursing, her breasts are flat. The reason a woman's breasts are permanently full-looking is to communicate the visual sign "I am female."

Since their frontal placement and hemispherical shape are hard to ignore, both men and women notice breasts. Bosoms arouse a man's eyes and stimulate his tactile sense. They signal sexual maturity and mothering, and suggest fertility. They are meaningful signs in courtship but not as significant as the face or hourglass figures. As ac-tress Audrey Hepburn proved, female beauty does not require notice-able breasts.

Contrary to popular opinion, cross-cultural research does not sup-port the notion that Western men have a breast fixation. Men every-where consider a shapely bosom attractive. In the Trobriand Islands of New Guinea, for example, where women do not cover their breasts, Trobriand men critique them with a keen eye. According to anthropologist Bronislaw Malinowski, author of *The Sexual Life of Savages*, *nutaviya* is the word for the full, firm, round breasts men prefer (Malinowski, 1929). *Nupipisiga* is the name for small, undeveloped, girlish breasts. Another native term likens flabby bosoms to "hanging ripe fruit." A fourth compares thin breasts to "aerial roots of the pandanus tree."

The torso itself is surprisingly variable in what people like and dislike. In the 1970s, an English study of men and women in their early to mid-twenties found that females with soft, round, endomorph figures—like those of *Venus de Milo* and Marilyn Monroe—were judged significantly more attractive than muscular mesomorphs or lean ectomorphs (Stewart et al., 1973). Today, all three body types seem to appeal. The long-limbed, narrow-shouldered, ectomorphic look of ballerinas, fashion models, and sinewy actresses like Calista Flockhart is attractive because it is more photogenic in magazines and on TV. The popularity of women's sports makes the wide-shouldered, narrow-hipped, mesomorphic look of gymnasts, tennis players, and singers like Madonna attractive as well.

Hips and the Bottom Line

Studies of human attractiveness find a slim waist "most attractive" in males and females (Horvath, 1979). For men rating women, attractiveness increases as waists narrow in relation to hip width. But hips judged "too narrow" are less attractive than hips judged "slightly too wide." Of course, hip size is easily adjusted with clothing.

In absolute terms, a woman's hips are bigger than a man's. Her pelvis is shorter but wider and deeper, and tilts farther forward than his. Her spine's S-shaped lumbar curve has a more visible inward arch to accent the roundness of her buttocks, which are set lower than a man's. What's more, her hip joint and her leg's *greater trochanter*, the projecting part of the upper leg bone, are wider, adding more breadth to her hips. A woman's abdomen is smoother and rounder, and her navel is more deeply set. Dramatically displayed by belly dancers, these feminine traits are featured around the world in the hula, the rumba, and the cancan.

Since hip movements in dance are suggestive of the pelvic girdle's rhythmic oscillations in lovemaking, their to-and-fro motions are universally provocative. In courtship, biological roots of hip displays run deep, as shown by the male guinea pig's precopulatory "rumba" dance. To be more attractive, he shifts his weight back and forth on his hind legs to rhythmically sway in front of a female (Bradbury and Vehrencamp, 1998).

Nowhere are human hips more tauntingly displayed than on MTV, the music channel. When men sing, women with bared thighs dance about them in high heels, their hips keeping time to the beat. When a woman sings, her own pelvis oscillates and sways with the melody. She rolls her hips as she walks toward the camera, and swings her bottom back and forth as she walks away. Facing forward again, she smiles, reaches her palm out, and juts out a hip.

The curvaceous human derrière is unique among primates. When we began walking upright four million years ago, *gluteus maximus* muscles changed position to give us true seats. Monkeys and apes have shapeless, essentially flat, seatless posteriors, but when a female comes into heat, her sexual skin swells with a visual sign of readiness to mate. To make sure he sees it, she presents her hindquarters for inspection.

In human beings after the age of twelve or thirteen, the female behind is continuously "swollen." Its shape and size emit a persistent gender message to male eyes. Women present their buttocks by bending forward, sitting in laps, or doing the cancan. Fashions from bustles to designer jeans accent the rounded shape of the female behind. Like breasts, a rounded backside connotes vulnerability and sends a tactile message: "I am touchable."

Just as men notice shapely bottoms. women appreciate a curvy male behind. Women consider pert. smaller buttocks the most physically attractive. Research shows that the least liked part of the male or female body is overly large buttocks.

The scientific study of physical differences between males and females began in 1871. In *The Descent of Man, and Selection in Relation to Sex*, Charles Darwin identified sexual selection as a force to be reckoned with in human evolution. Sexual selection, he found, worked in tandem with his better known principle of natural selection. In the 1970s, sexual selection became a lively research area and continues as a key subfield of biology to this day. It includes the study of secondary sexual traits and the role of male and female choice in selecting a mate. Thanks to what scientists have learned since Darwin's time, we now understand how gender differences attract.

In the next chapter I discuss ways to optimize natural gender cues through the uniquely human invention of clothing. The leopard cannot change its spots to be more appealing in courtship, but we can and do.

9. CLOTHING AND ADORNMENT: DRESS TO OBSESS

Forget that old hippie saying, you are what you eat.
In the modern world, you are what you wear.
—SUZY GERSHMAN

Clothing should always move with your body.
Fashion is an extension of body language. A new garment
creates a new posture—and a new attitude—
in its wearer.
—VÉRONIQUE VIENNE

IN COURTSHIP, CLOTHING and adornment are all about controlling the eye of the beholder. You bedeck your body with lines, spots, textures, colors, and contrasts to bring eyes upward to your face, downward to your feet and ankles, and sideward to your shoulders, wrists, and hands. By marking your best features with eye-catching designs, fabrics, and accessories, you bring attention directly to them—and simultaneously divert eyes from the body's less flattering parts. Your choice of lapels, collars, buttons, sleeves, cuffs, and shoes powerfully influences how others perceive and relate to you. Are you an individual, an artist, a cowpoke, or a corporate clone? Any or all of these personas can be attractive in courtship. The main question is, will you leave a lasting impression or be left in the crowd?

The Librarian's Tale

Every day she rides home on the 5:10 express from the school where she works as a librarian. Every day it's the same seat—halfway back on the right—and the same clothing style. The librarian's neutral-toned, workaday outfit is a study in plainness. She has on a beige turtleneck sweater, a beige raincoat, beige slacks, and light brown sensible shoes with plain brown laces.

For makeup, she has two patches of blush on her cheeks. She wears no mascara, eyebrow pencil, or lipstick. There are BB-size gold earrings attached to her earlobes. A short, wire-tight perm sits on her head like a cap, and glasses with putty-colored frames round out the picture. Even though she has a pleasing face and an hourglass figure, few men would court her. Beige Dewey decimal, sack-cloth-and-ashes academic, her costume says, "Pass me by."

And they do. It goes without saying that many men are less than attentive observers of how women dress. At lower brain levels, however, in subconscious modules of the limbic system, where they make courting decisions, little escapes their "notice." Men sense when a woman dresses to be seen and when she dresses to hide, because her clothing speaks a nonverbal language their emotions understand.

The Attraction of Blue Jeans

Had the librarian wanted attention, she would have worn something other than beige. Alone, the light gray, yellowish-brown color is tiresome, unexciting, and plain. Dressing all in beige makes a person seem conservative, passive, and neutral. Beige is a common background color for corporate walls, and beige clothing keeps wearers similarly out of sight, unnoticed, and in the background.

To enhance visibility, consider the color blue. Unlike beige, blue strongly attracts the eye. Like our monkey and ape relatives, we have a gene that specifically encodes for blue-light-sensitive pigments. Indigo blue dye has been found in prehistoric cave paintings and was used to color wool four thousand years ago. Today blue, along with red, is the most popular adult favorite color. Symbolically, blue stands for tenderness and truth. Psychologically, blue communicates a pleasant, secure, and tender mood.

An appealing fabric for courtship, worn by men and women around the world, is blue denim. As denim cloth fades, it takes on the mood-elevating pastel hues of a clear blue sky. We perceive Levi's© sky-blue color as cheery, accessible, and "friendly." Highly diluted by white, faded denim evokes amicable feelings in viewers and makes it easier for them to approach. Pastel clothing is more congenial than assertive, primary-colored clothes, which seem to leap forward and shout for attention.

The homespun look and crumpled texture of denim's twill weave create an "easygoing" fabric with a decidedly casual fashion statement. Visually and in the tactile mode, denim's coarseness opposes the formality of creased trousers and pressed slacks. Dressing down in Levi's© sends an unassuming message that puts viewers instantly at ease. A subtle message also comes from the tiny red tag situated on a wearer's right buttock. Marking it with crimson, the small but conspicuous scarlet label brings attention to the derrière.

Ever since the 1955 movie *Rebel Without a Cause*, blue jeans have been tailored to showcase a wearer's behind. In studio posters for *Rebel*, James Dean displayed his hindquarters as he stood with his back turned and his hands thrust into his jeans' back pockets. If Dean were any other primate than a human, we would say he was presenting his bottom as monkeys and apes present theirs for sexual display. Turning his vulnerable backside, Dean sent a suggestive message to signify "I'm accessible."

Presenting hindquarters in blue jeans became fashionable in 1977, when fifteen-year-old Brooke Shields bent over to advertise her Calvin

Klein jeans. Among primates, the curvilinear human behind is a unique nonverbal cue born of muscles for upright posture (the gluteus maximus) and, in females, of adipose fatty tissue stored for childbirth. Brooke's magazine ads graphically affirmed the power of blue jeans in courtship. The teenage model answered her own flirtatious question—"You know what comes between me and my Calvin's?"—with a coy response: "Nothing."

According to NASA, the mean buttock circumference in men is 39.2 inches and in women, 37.4 inches. Women have fuller, rounder bottoms, but the derrières of both sexes may be fashionably displayed in blue jeans. A woman's form-fitting jeans cling to the curves of her buttocks, thighs, kneecaps, and calves. A man's relaxed, loose-fitting jeans visually enhance the thickness of his upper and lower legs. In men's and women's jeans, a prominent vertical line defined by the zipper shield, in tandem with horizontal furrows that gather above the jean's high inseams, guide eyes to the pivotal juncture where legs and pelvis meet at the crotch. Visually, this intimate bodily area is more conspicuous in jeans than in dresses, skirts, or trousers with a lower inseam.

Nonverbal signs encoded in pants, skirts, tops, belts, jewelry, footwear, hats, and tattoos add telling reference points to your upright, bipedal frame. As anthropologist Edward Hall noted, body-adornment messages broadcast continuously as "frozen gestures." Squaring the torso with shoulder pads affirms a self-assured posture throughout the day. A vertical necktie "lifts" your face and chin. A beret worn at an angle gives your head a friendly tilt to one side. A smiley-face emblem worn on a T-shirt makes you seem friendly all day. Gestures encoded in clothing carry credible information about your age, gender, social status, sexual orientation, and state of mind—and about your unspoken desire to be hidden or seen. The fashion choices you make in courtship are endless, but like an actor choosing how to play a role, you decide.

Does the Shoe Fit?

Nothing you wear is more expressive than footwear. "Shoes hold the key to human identity," says Sonja Bata, founder of Toronto's Bata Shoe Museum. In matters of courtship, footwear plays a sensual role. A shoe's secret message stems from the curious anatomical fact that our feet and sexual organs border each other on the parietal lobe's sensory strip. Since the tactile mappings of feet and genitalia meet in the brain, touching the former suggests touching the latter. Feet are similarly shy, sensitive, ticklish, and sexy, and we display them in footwear as if they were our private fetishes.

Evidence from prehistory supports the claim that everyone has a shoe fetish.

Human beings have been decorating their sandals and shoes since the beginning of the Neolithic Age ten thousand years ago. According to archaeologists who found them in homes, tombs, and ancient burial sites, the earliest sandals came in hundreds of designs. Style in footwear was important from the very beginning, and today's shoes have a great deal to say about your goals and objectives in courtship.

Feminine footwear shows personality and uniqueness as if to say "I'm someone special." A man's footwear is part of a uniform marking membership in a group. Masculine shoes say, "I'm a jock," "I'm an urban cowboy," or "I'm on the management team."

Women's Shoe Secrets

For women, the most attractive shoes are "revealing." Sandals with thin ankle straps strategically bare the toes, heels, ankles, and tops of the feet or insteps. Revealing shoes call attention to thinner bones, smaller joints, and delicate Achilles tendons. The male eye is tempted by slim, curvilinear ankles ascending from low-cut pumps or high heels, and by peep-toes revealing toe cleavage between the first and second digits. Clear plastic evening sandals with three-inch heels and thin black straps artfully showcase exposed feminine toes which seem, in their petiteness and vulnerability, childlike and cute. Since revealing shoes are submissive and give power away, they should not be worn in the boardroom.

Men also like close-fitting, binding shoes which cover a woman's feet while enhancing their silhouetted contour. With taut laces, a binding shoe's snug fit transmits suggestive messages of tight containment. Anthropologist Alan Dundee thinks binding shoes encode an implicit sexual meaning: "The foot fitting in the shoe—you have the act, the same as putting a finger through a ring. There's some actual iconic representations of the sexual act here" (Kastor, 1994:30).

Familiar binding shoes include the ankle-high, buttoned boots of the 1900s; 1970s mid-calf boots cut close to the leg; and the tight patent-leather, ankle-high shoes worn by pop singer Madonna in the 1980s. Tall, tight-fitting suede boots with semi-high heels and belt-and-buckle accents across the instep are effective in courtship today. In such "containment" styles, the medium is the manacle.

For an appealing look, trade in your flats for high heels. Even slightly elevated heels enhance the shape of your bottom, firm your lower legs, and showcase your ankles. Heels add an ethereal quality by making your body seem to rise and defy Earth's gravitational pull. Aesthetically, heels also make your legs look longer in proportion to body size. Through the biological principle of *mimicry*, legs in high heels resemble the youthful, slim legs of an eighteen-year-old.

High heels position wearers precariously up on their tiptoes. This shifts the body's center of gravity forward, causing a compensatory forward lean. Already prominent by primate standards, the buttocks protrude an additional 25 percent. Both high heels and cowboy boots cause the rear end to project. Wearing heels contracts both heads of the calf, or *gastrocnemius*, muscle to slim and firm the back of the lower leg. Meanwhile, ankles ride prominently high in the shoes for all to see. So stunning is the overall effect that heels will likely never go out of style.

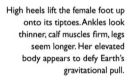

High heels lift the female foot up onto its tiptoes. Ankles look thinner, calf muscles firm, legs seem longer. Her elevated body appears to defy Earth's gravitational pull.

Shoe Voodoo

An optical illusion makes female feet more petite-looking in "Chanel-style" shoes. Launched in the 1950s by Coco Chanel, the light-colored woman's shoe came with a distinctive black toe cap. Contrast between the shoe and its darker toe box made for a deceptively smaller foot. Chanel shoes illusively extended the vertical length of the legs to make them look "thinner" as well. Though the classic Chanel is dated, visual principles encoded in its design are found in many women's shoes today. Chanel-style shoes magically "shrink" the foot from one to three sizes at a glance.

Men's Shoes Show Strength

Shoes are one of the first things a woman notices. A becoming style for men in courtship is the stomping shoe. This psychologically dominant brand of footwear is designed to enhance masculine size, strength, and swagger. It is typified by thick, crepe-sole beetle crushers worn by English Teddy boys of the 1950s, by middle-class desert boots of the 1950s and '60s, by urbane Timberland boots of the 1970s, and by aggressive Doc Marten boots worn by young men and women today. Men's oxford, brogue, and saddle-shoe styles are also heavily soled. Dominant styles are robust—wide, thick, and heavy— to accent the size of the foot and its ability to stomp. Not that he (or she) needs to, of course, but the symbolism is there to behold.

The oldest stomping shoes are sandals from ancient Egypt with pictures of enemies painted on their soles. Today, if tying a shoelace is a learned activity, stomping is innate. Even blind- and deaf-born children stamp their feet in anger, according to biologist Irenaus Eibl-Eibesfeldt. Foot stomping, he adds, evolved as a "ritualized attack movement" (Eibl-Eibesfeldt, 1970:96). The sight of a stomping shoe puts the brain stem on alert with its subliminal aggressive message. On a subconscious level, we alert to thick-soled boots and the masculine dangers they portend. Boots signify power, and as Nobel Peace Prize–winner Henry Kissinger said, "Power is the ultimate aphrodisiac."

By popularizing thick, buckled motorcycle boots, Marlon Brando in *The Wild One* (1954) and Peter Fonda in *Easy Rider* (1969) furthered the role of footwear as a fashion statement designed to figuratively "stomp" the powers-that-be. Boots suggest strength by increasing one's vertical height and psychological stature. They give a more powerful gait and add stability for a more commanding stance. A boot shaft's snug contact with pressure-sensitive *Pacinian corpuscles* of the lower leg provides tactile reassurance and supports the long tendons that drop into feet from muscles above. Boots also stabilize the ankle joints. By adapting to the physical needs of our feet—and to our reptilian brain's psychic need for power—Doc Martens help us stand taller, look stronger, and feel more secure in nightspots of the urban jungle.

Also attractive to women, but with a softer sell in courtship, is a man's "mincing" shoe. This is a submissive, narrow style, with lightweight uppers, thin soles, and tapering toes. Classic mincing shoes include the pointed "winkle-pickers" worn by British mods of the 1950s, pointy-toed Beatle boots of the 1960s, and the slipperlike Gucci loafer of today. Tassel slip-ons, Hush Puppies, and Italian shoes by Lorenzo Banfi are typical of this less-threatening style of footwear, which downplays the male foot's clumsy size and bluntness. With their slimmer, narrower, more vulnerable look, gracile shoes connote a mood of receptiveness and sensitivity.

His and Hers Sneakers

Like boots, high heels, and mincing shoes, sneakers have much to say in courtship. Sneakers were popularized by James Dean in *Guys and Dolls* (1955) and by Elvis Presley's teen cohort in *Jailhouse Rock* (1957). Sneakers broke the formality of corporate leather shoes to express a kinder, gentler world for the feet and the casual lifestyle for which they stand.

Bold lines and color contrasts in running, training, and sports shoes betoken youth and physical fitness (often more theatrical than real). In courtship, sneakers hold the promise of energy and enthusiasm. The pliable nylon upper and soft, thick sole of latex or vinyl demonstrate a fondness for informality and comfort over fashion and style.

Véronique Vienne, author of *The Art of the Moment*, advises that sneakers should determine the look of the

clothes you're going to wear—not the other way around
(Vienne. 1997).

In tandem with its eye-catching sports insignia, crisscrossing lines, and curvilinear swooshes, a sneaker's whiteness brings eyes directly to the feet and their suggestive nuances. With half-inch-thick soles, sneakers give wearers an endearing "clumsy" walk suggestive of childhood. Less coordination and *savoir faire* are communicated by bouncy sneakers than by a thin-soled shoe's smoother gait. It's the difference between a child's mittens and kidskin gloves.

Quite often *People* and *Us* magazines run photos of celebrity couples in look-alike sneakers strolling the streets of Hollywood and L.A. In matching sneakers, they feel psychologically alike through the principle of isopraxism. Sportswear is action oriented, and couples connect by matching each other's stride in the same athletic footwear. They walk, as it were, in each other's shoes.

Wearing sneakers to bring out the child in you is always attractive in courtship.

Leg Signals

Of vital importance in courtship is how you structure the form and content of the space between your shoes and waistline. Adornment in this area is designed to cover, modify, or accent the color, thickness, length, shape, taper, and texture of your legs. For best results, leg signals should be carefully coordinated with messages emanating from footwear below. Since cuffed trousers widen the legs, they go better with heavy shoes to anchor the stability of a man's stance. With skirts that bare the curve of hose-clad calves, heels work better to levitate a woman above the earthly plane.

For decades in movies—while fleeing from gorillas, giant lizards,

or martians—leading men in pants and boots came to the aid of leading ladies in skirts and heels, as the latter twisted their ankles, stum-
bled, and fell to the ground. Times have changed, and today's women
star in commanding action roles like that of Angelina Jolie in *Tomb
Raider* and Cameron Diaz in *Charlie's Angels*. This reflects a novel trend
in courtship toward androgyny, as young women behave more like
men, and vice versa. As would be expected, burgeoning parity between the sexes is reflected in clothing.

Generation-X men and women, born between 1965 and 1979, are
more androgynous in the way they dress than are Baby Boomers or
elders of the *Ozzie & Harriet* era. In the latter cohorts, males and females dress differently to magnify their gender contrasts. Generation
X dresses to minimize them. Like Gen-X males, Gen-X females wear
sandals, sneakers, clogs, and thick-soled shoes or boots with T-shirts,
tank tops, and blue jeans. By dressing, talking, and acting alike in
courtship, men and women of this generation feel close through isopraxism's credo of same behavior. Traveling, hiking, and adventuring
together—sharing bottled water, energy drinks, and Mountain Dew—
unites them as allies in the cohort.

Our species is unlikely ever to adopt a thoroughly unisex outlook
in courtship. Clothing styles change, but differentiating the sexes stays
the same. To distinguish themselves in androgynous apparel, Gen-X
women fashionably bare midriffs, hips, and lower backs with drop-
waist pants and truncated, short-shirt tops; bare ankles with higher
pant cuffs; bare toes with open-front shoes and sandals; and showcase
navels with piercings. Gen-X men keep these body parts covered,
thankfully, out of sight and mind.

Gen-X men cut their hair close to the scalp, erect bangs in jaunty
topknots, and wear baseball caps with lowered bills to suggest larger
masculine brows, or *superciliary ridges*. Since male and female roles are
basically conserved in courtship, they remain visibly distinctive. Even
in Hollywood—which sets the tone for generational deportment with

music videos, ads, and MTV—male and female clothing stereotypes rule today as they did in 1942, when Bogart and Bergman courted in *Casablanca.*

The most attractive leg wear for women is still the classic, leg-displaying skirt. According to archaeologists, the oldest-known skirt was already provocative and revealing in its day. Evidence for the ancient "string skirt" consists of detailed carvings on Upper Paleolithic Venus figurines from Lespugue, France, estimated to be twenty-three to twenty-five thousand years old. The erotic string skirt, which resembles the hula skirt of old Hawaii, revealed the legs and ankles, and made sexually suggestive swaying movements as women walked (Barber, 1994).

Prehistoric man may have enjoyed the string skirt's swing and sway more than the sight of an unclothed body. Evidence from a well-studied South Pacific culture at least supports the notion. In traditional Guadalcanal society, both sexes went naked until puberty, at which time they wore a pandanus-palm leaf or strip of bark cloth tied with string around the waist, but a Guadalcanal prostitute wore a full grass skirt to enhance her bodily charms. "To be provocative," anthropologist Ian Hogbin writes, "she wore a short grass skirt and many ornaments; and she spent her time bathing and rubbing her limbs with fragrant oil" (Hogbin, 1964:20).

A flared long dress accents a woman's walk with sensuous, undulating movements that catch the eye and suggest a graceful bearing. Like an ice dancer, she "floats" through space seemingly unencumbered by gravity's pull.

Since women are not as obsessed by bare limbs, the best leg wear for today's man would be pants. Trousers mask a man's hairier skin while suggesting that he treads seriously and solidly upon the earth. In tandem with heavy footwear, masculine cuffs define a solid connection with terra firma, as if he had both feet on the ground. Connotations of masculine "solidity" make pants fashionable in courtship around the world, even in lands where ceremonial kilts, kimonos, and sarongs are worn.

Discovered on a glacier between Austria and Italy, the oldest-known trousers were crotchless animal-hide leggings worn with a leather loincloth. They belonged to a late-Neolithic wanderer known as the Ice Man who died 5,300 years ago. The deerskin pants covering his thighs and calves did not cling but had a loose fit to enable bending at the knees. An artist's rendering of his leather cuffs and shoes suggests that, unlike top-heavy Venus figurines, whose legs taper to an unstable, pointed tip, the Ice Man's leg wear provided a stable platform upon which to stand.

In their evolution as consumer products, trousers signify a more active lifestyle than that betokened by lava-lavas and skirts. Men's pants show an Indo-European design of equestrian origin. According to archaeologist Elizabeth Barber, trousers as we know them now were invented two thousand years ago to keep the tender parts of a man from chafing as he rode horseback on the steppes. As Barber writes, "The man's chemise was then shortened (*shirt* means 'cut short') to allow the straddling position" (Barber, 1994:142). In clothing for horsemanship or courtship, form follows function.

THE HIDDEN PERSUADERS IN YOUR WARDROBE

- Open your collar to show the neck dimple's *suprasternal notch*. Exposing this physically weak body part invites attention and makes you seem more available, approachable, and open.
- Your top's colors and contrasts should mimic the basic colors and contrasts of your skin, eyes, and hair. Your face is most

CONTINUED ON NEXT PAGE

attractive when you wear a blouse, jacket, or shawl that echoes its pigments to create a clear gestalt. Chestnut shades resonate with dark hair and brown eyes. Off-white picks up lighter hair and skin tones.

- Your body is relentlessly bilateral. Wear an asymmetrical item, like a pocket square, a flower pinned to the left lapel, or a hair clip on the right to make yourself more noticeable.
- Raise or lower your jacket's waist button to define the proper balance between leg length and torso height. A lowered button balances longer legs. A raised button "lengthens" legs that look short in relation to an elongated torso.
- If you are very thin, add horizontal lines with pocket flaps, cuffs, and wide lapels to widen your frame.
- Wear stockings the same shade as shoes to suggest proportionally longer legs.
- Choose a collar size and shape to flatter the size and shape of your face. Long faces attract well in wide collars with blunt points. Round faces attract in narrow collars with projecting points.
- Wear touchable tweed, cashmere, flannel, silk, suede, lace, or knitted weaves to stimulate touch-sensitive neurons in your partner's sensory cortex. Touchable textures say, "Please touch."
- In-curving lines of a fitted jacket flatter the waistline. They create an indented hourglass shape above a woman's hips. Hidden beneath a jacket's hemline, full hips look "smaller."
- Three-quarter-length sleeves make a woman's fingers look "longer" beneath exposed forearms.
- If you are very tall, a jacket with lower-sitting lapels makes you look shorter.
- Wide shoulders on a jacket make your head look smaller. Narrow shoulders make it look bigger.

The Right Arm Signals

Arm wear is clothing worn to cover, expose, or modify the color, thickness, length, and shape of your arms. It also includes the tattoos, ornaments, bracelets, and wristbands you wear to attract notice, and to mark masculine or feminine gender. What you place upon your arms accents their thickness or taper. A flannel shirt adds masculine bulk to the biceps area, while a short-sleeve blouse reveals the slimness, length, and grace of feminine arms, hands, and fingers. Arm wear also influences body movement. As tailors know, the fit of a sleeve defines how you bend over and reach.

The most attractive arm wear for a woman with thin limbs is little or no apparel on the arms. Men are attracted by slim upper arms and forearms, and by the curvilinear shape of deltoid muscles, biceps, and flexed wrists. When her wrist is bent, the subcutaneous layer of fatty tissue makes a woman's wrist rounder and smoother than a man's.

Despite the popularity of tank tops and sleeveless tees, the most attractive arm wear for a man in courtship is long sleeves. Deprived of his coat of mammalian fur, the average man's bared arms look rather thin and exposed. In the workplace, he keeps them covered for more powerful leverage on the job. A business jacket's thick sleeves inflate the authority of biceps, forearms, and wrists. A sports coat defines an image of exalted physical strength. We have faith in these grand illusions because primate eyes trust what they see.

In courtship, even a bodybuilder's arms look better under cover. We have seen that women are intimidated by overly muscled physiques. If the message of huge biceps is blatant, the suggestion of strength connoted by a cardigan sweater's bulky sleeves attractively understates the case with its temperate message: "I am strong but constrained within close bounds."

Sleeves cut full at the top of a man's upper arm should taper downward to his wrist. This adds a graceful line suggesting there's more to the man than arm strength. Sleeves that flap about the wrists seem awkward and take attention from masculine hands.

MARK YOUR BODY WITH NATURAL ACCESSORIES

The shape, sheen, hue, and texture of natural substances bring attention to the natural tones, textures, and colors of your skin and hair. Strategically placed amber, coral, silver, gold, or pearl jewelry draws eyes and creates memorable impact:

- **Amber** brings attention with a lustrous golden glow. Made from once-living tree sap, amber has been considered magical since Upper Paleolithic times. Prominently worn at midline on the chest as a pendant, amber makes a dramatic statement and draws eyes upward to your neck and face.
- Tiny faces carved in coral, onyx, or shell **cameos** bring instant notice. Eyes alert to faces through dedicated temporal-lobe modules programmed to notice facial gestalts. Worn on the neck or just below the neckline, a cameo's carved facial features resonate with your features above.
- **Coral** attracts eyes with a pink, salmon, or oxblood-red color. Worn below the shoulder, a coral pin creates an asymmetry that resonates well with dark hair and eyes. Coral earrings add eye-catching focal points at the sides of your face, and pick up the blush of rosy cheeks.
- A **gold** necklace draws eyes with its gleaming shine. Reflecting light onto your skin, the necklace adds a curvilinear border to your lower face. In tandem with the hairline's top border, your face is attractively framed and highlighted. Yellow gold flatters every skin tone, and its sparkle picks up the gleam of sparkling eyes.
- **Silver** has a pale, luminous sheen. Worn as a bracelet, it may be echoed with small silver earrings to reinforce the display. Silver's smooth surface reflects the smoothness of skin.
- The satin-white glow of **pearls** brings out your skin's natural glow. Pearl earrings bring eyes back and forth across your face. Their spherical shape recalls the roundness of irises and eyes.

Shoulder Wear

Flat-lying shoulders stand out as conspicuous shapes set high and wide upon your frame. How you clothe them affects what they have to say. So expressive are shoulders in courtship that distinctive clothing has evolved in every society to accent their messages. Clothing worn on or about the shoulders accents gestures derived from two vertebrate-wide status displays, the high stand of dominance and the crouch of submission. Suit jackets square, while décolleté blouses bare, the shoulders to show, respectively, the strength of a broadside or the softness of a shrug.

For a woman, flattering shoulder wear shows off the shoulders themselves and reveals their emotional responses. The best clothing bares one or both shoulders, accentuates their rounded shape, and allows freedom of movement. Revealed shoulders send potent messages of femininity. Baring one shoulder adds an eye-catching asymmetry to the female frame. Puffy sleeves keep a woman's shoulders permanently "shrugged." The frozen gesture says, "I am harmless; you may approach." In paintings from antiquity, Egyptian women wear tubular, ankle-length jumpers with shoulder straps. The splendor of arms, shoulders, and collarbones shows through the ages.

Contemporary women's wear beckons with the same cues. Sleeveless sweaters and blouses display rounded deltoids. U-neck, V-neck, boat-neck, and scoop-neck tops reveal the collarbone beneath the neck dimple. Though upstaged by breasts, these feminine body parts are highly visible and very attractive to the male eye. A surplice-wrap dress forms a deep V over the clavicle and breastbone, or *sternum*, and a camisole's straps add lines to draw eyes outward across the shoulders' exposed skin. Fabrics such as taffeta, velvet, velour, and silk mimic the softness of shoulders, adding to their call.

A smooth, well-pressed top makes your face look smoother. A wrinkled shirt or blouse adds lines that echo facial creases and make your face look older.

A U-neck top is kinder and gentler than a sharper V-neck. Psychologically, rounded lines are more feminine and yielding than the unbending shapes of angular necklines.

For a man, the best shoulder wear features strength cues from the vertebrate's broadside display. To appear physically powerful, men and male animals flaunt expanded versions of themselves to loom larger than they are in fact. Business, military, and sports jackets enlarge shoulder breadth and height as they widen chests. Just as puffer fish balloon in size to show deceptively broader profiles, a man's flaring lapels make him loom larger on the scene. Women are more likely to cast jacketed "big men" in protector roles.

Color Consciousness

Primates exhibit the most conspicuous sex differences in coloration of all mammals, and humans are no exception to the rule. In courtship, colors make an outfit come alive with feeling. A red blouse is exciting and sexually provocative. A green shirt seems laid back and leisurely. Yellow stands out in a crowd, and yellow-on-black is the most visible color contrast known to man. Fiery orange is the color of rebels who dare to be different. Blue is cool and collected; purple connotes sadness; brown is emotionally blah. Since no hue escapes from its dark surface, black is the most mysterious color. Black hides emotion as sunglasses hide eyes, as if to say, "Keep your distance." Friendly white speaks of innocence and approachability, but the

friendliest tops in courtship are pink. Pink signals the brain's hypothalamus to slow adrenal secretions and check stranger anxiety.

Monochromatic black seems pure, hard, and impersonal.
It was the favorite color of abstract expressionist
painter Ad Reinhardt, the quintessential minimalist who re-
duced reality to absolute darkness. Dressing all in black
brings absolute attention to your face.

Invented nine thousand years ago, cloth changed courtship forever.
Woven cloth became an indispensable means for advertising femininity and masculinity, rivaling the body itself as a medium of expression.
Clothing communicates moods and feelings as powerfully as gestures
alone did in the remote past. Clearly, fashion has become the new
body language of boy-meets-girl. In courtship, you are what you wear.
Controlling where others look, you control what they see.

10. SPACES, PLACES, AND INTERIORS

As a rule, a span of three bar stools is the
maximum distance over which patrons will
attempt to initiate an encounter.
—MARK L. KNAPP

FROM YOUR FOUR-STAR restaurant's window table, amid an ornate, pastel décor filled with the fragrance of roses and fine linen, you gaze at sparkling big-city lights and agree: this place definitely has it. Feasting on continental cuisine in a smaller, apricot-and-pale-green room trimmed with bright floral bouquets, you perceive: this bistro has it, too. Tantalizing foreign menus, soft lights, elegant furnishings . . . "it" all adds up to the same ineffable thing: romance.

As anthropologist Edward Hall observed, "Space speaks." The physical setting against which courtship takes place can help or hinder couples far more subtly than they realize. Although roses and violins do engender in some of us a magical, romantic mood, the "right place at the right time" can turn out to be anything from a quiet cafeteria to a music-filled Hard Rock Café.

Its musical beat makes the bustling Hard Rock—with establishments around the world from Atlanta to Bali—a better venue for courtship than restaurants with roses-and-violins themes. Research suggests that the Hard Rock's throbbing music can actually make you "nicer looking." In a study of the effects of background music on physical attractiveness, researchers found that women who listened to rock music rated photos of men more attractive than they did without the lively background beat (May and Hamilton, 1980). Without music (or while listening only to background jazz), women judged the photographs significantly less attractive.

Sit with the Beautiful People

With or without mood music, studies show that you are nicer looking when you sit near people who are physically attractive themselves. The "glitter" phenomenon—what social psychologists call the *association effect*—made its scientific debut in the 1930s in a watershed study by sociologist Willard Waller (1937) on "The Rating and Dating Complex." Today, corroborated by researchers for decades, the association effect is an immutable law of psychology. It holds true for both sexes, irrespective of the relationship each has, or does not have, with the good-looking others. Just being physically near them is the key. Whenever possible, sit close to, and position your date's chair to face, the beautiful people.

Bubbles in Space

Whether you choose to meet in elegant four-star surroundings or in corner cafés, your first problem is coping with the unseen dimensions of *personal space*. As the Swiss artist Alberto Giacometti graphically depicted, the distinction between your body and the space it inhabits is blurred. In Giacometti's portraits of Stravinsky, Sartre, and Matisse, bodily edges seem to dissolve into the surrounding canvas. And, indeed, the human person does not stop at skin level but radiates outward in invisible zones. An enclosing, emotionally charged envelope of personal space encircles each one of us, and only selected "safe" partners are allowed entrance.

Scientific research on how we communicate in public places began with studies of animal behavior and territoriality in the late nineteenth and early twentieth centuries. Later, in the mid-twentieth century, Edward Hall popularized spatial research on human beings—calling it *proxemics*—in his book *The Silent Language* (1959). Today, much of what we know about love's silent language concerns matters of interpersonal space.

Hall discovered a clear envelope that surrounds our body like a bubble. Known as *personal distance*, this invisible, untouchable, odorless, and silent sheath has a concentric, layered structure not unlike that of a sliced boiled egg. Hall identified four bodily distances—*intimate* (0 to 18 inches), *personal* (1.5 to 4 feet), *social* (4 to 10 feet), and *public* (10 feet and beyond)—as key zones in the spacing behavior of adults from the American Northeast.

A cultural anthropologist, Hall noted that different groups set distinctive dimensions for each of the four proxemic zones. In the early stages of courtship, French and Italian couples tend to establish physically closer comfort zones than American, German, or British pairs. Sitting or standing too close or too far away from a partner leads to misunderstandings and can bring on the confusion and anxiety anthropologists know as *culture shock*. That a Saudi's space envelope is smaller than an American's may lead to discomfort. A native Texas woman may feel trapped talking to a Saudi man whose face looms closer than 18 inches, while he may feel snubbed should she step back or angle away. Bubble size varies, but in all societies the intimate zone is reserved for close friends, family, and lovers.

In every culture, the encapsulating sheath extends farther in front than out to the sides. Experiments show that a head-on advance from someone unknown is likely to produce mild to moderate feelings of apprehension, which prompt defensive postures like turning the face and body away to one side. Skin-conductance tests reveal that palms sweat significantly more—a telltale sign of stranger anxiety—in a direct, frontal approach.

Studies show that men feel less invaded when approached from the side. Women prefer friendly approaches from the front.

Since our bubble of personal space balloons more in front than to the left or right, an effective ploy in courtship is to move toward someone obliquely from the side in a "slant" pattern. This unobtrusive approach, known as *sidling*, is useful in the early stages of a relationship to minimize stranger anxiety. Sidling, defined as "an unobtrusive or coy advance," is most appropriately used by women. Studies suggest that men feel less invaded when approached from the side. Men, however, may not find sidling as effective in courtship as a straight-ahead approach. Research shows that women prefer friendly approaches from the front.

Women seem less threatening when they advance toward a man's right side. In right-handed men (90 percent of all males), the right side of the body is less emotional than the left. (For left-handed men the situation is likely to be reversed.) Controlled by his analytic left brain, a man's right flank feels less exposed than its counterpart on the other side. Controlled by the emotional right brain, his left flank is more easily startled by a stranger's advance.

Invading the intimate zone of a woman's face may provoke a sudden head turn away, compressed lips, and tensed shoulders. Seeing these defensive cues, a man should withdraw to her less-guarded personal zone, 2 to 4 feet away. In dealings with strangers, women tolerate closer distances with unknown females than with unacquainted males. Unless her body language clearly invites him closer, a man should keep an arm's length away, on the outskirts of her *flight distance*. From this point in space, he would need to step forward before actually touching. According to zoologist Heini Hediger, crossing the invisible threshold of flight distance—where he could reach out and touch without taking a step—arouses protective emotions that could lead her to take wing.

W omen seem less threatening when they advance toward a man's right-hand side, because it is emotionally less sensitive than his body's left.

At close quarters, men and women respond to different facial cues. Men find it easier approaching women who keep their eyes averted than those who look directly back and smile. Females, on the other hand, more easily approach males who smile and gaze back into their eyes. Men are more likely to show clear signs of annoyance should a woman overstep her bounds. Her invasion may trigger visible tightening in his lips and a step backward. Studies find, conversely, that women suffer in silence. Which is to say, women show less obvious unease when men loom too close. Since he may not receive clear cues about her boundary lines, a man should keep his distance until he receives an explicit welcoming sign: a smile, a head tilt to the side, or a beckoning glance from under her lashes.

Gender differences also show in seating arrangements. Between strangers in a pub or espresso bar, a man should sit directly across from a woman. This position is less threatening than sitting down beside her. For men the opposite is true: A man feels calmer when a woman sits to his side rather than directly in front, where significant eye contact takes place. This is counterproductive from his perspective, of course, since a man's eyes top a woman's most-attractive list. All is not logical in courtship, and it's easier to start a conversation when you respect the unwritten rules of personal space.

Unwritten Rules of Personal Space

Personal space is the area immediately surrounding your body that you claim as your private territory. When someone inadvertently enters this space without permission, you feel emotionally upset. Overstepping a partner's invisible boundary lines can end a courtship before it begins.

- Avoid physical contact while speaking to casual acquaintances. While some find a preemptive touch to the back, arm, or shoulder pleasing, it's a relationship breaker for most. Since they seriously infringe upon personal space, uninvited pats, taps, and nudges are always risky in courtship.
- Watch for warning signs that you are physically too close. Your partner will suddenly look away to the right or left, compress lips, cross arms, lean to one side, angle away, or step back.
- When a partner steps back, do not step forward to close the gap. Defer to the unspoken need for personal space.
- At a table, a woman feels relaxed when a man sits across from rather than beside her. With her hair styled and face made up, she feels more empowered facing a partner directly than she does sitting to the side.
- A man feels relaxed when a woman sits beside him. Conversationally less skilled and facially less expressive, he may feel insecure chatting face-to-face with a new partner. The best strategy for a woman is to begin a conversation at his side and then move to the more forward position.
- Until invited, do not reach arms or fingers inside the intimate zone. Keep hand gestures below a partner's chin to avoid the sensitive "flinch" area in front of the face, nose, and eyes.
- If you are seriously taller, heavier, louder, or dressed in bright colors, you loom closer in your partner's eyes. Step back to leave a little more room. If you are shorter, smaller, softer-voiced, or dressed in muted shades, you may stand a few inches closer than the rules allow.

- Avoid being a "close talker." A close talker is an annoying person, usually a man, who doesn't understand the spatial boundaries of a conversation. Speaking in uncomfortably close proximity—nearer than 18 inches—makes him seem pushy and "in your face."

The odds of starting a conversation in a coffee bar or nightclub vary in proportion to the linear distance separating patrons. Anthropologist Mark Knapp observed that we are unlikely to converse over a span of four or more bar stools. Space permitting, a man should leave an empty stool—a spatial buffer—between himself and the partner he addresses. When the conversation takes, he should occupy the vacant seat to keep rival males from invading. Knapp found "seat changing" to be a typically male practice in courtship. For females, maneuvering closer too soon is a mistake because it prematurely telegraphs her feelings. His forward move, on the other hand, like the approach of a bull moose, is a proprietary signal given to keep competitors away. It speaks less of romance and more about territory.

COLORS TO DINE BY

Eating together is a universal theme in human courtship. Food stimulates the nervous system's rest-and-digest response to relieve fight-or-flight impulses aroused by the presence of strangers. The rest-and-digest principle helps couples relax as they dine. Since the color scheme of a restaurant, café, or fast-food interior affects your date's comfort level, you should be as mindful of where you eat as of what you order.

McDonald's stark yellow-and-red décor prompts you to dine in haste. High illumination and bold, primary colors overstimulate vision centers so a pair feels neither like resting and digesting nor like staying and chatting. Saturated reds reflexively

CONTINUED ON NEXT PAGE

raise blood pressure and increase muscle tension by as much as 80 percent (Birren, 1978).

With its muted color scheme of brown, off-white, pale yellow, and rose, a Denny's helps you relax, linger, and visit. Couples find it easier chatting in tranquil environments marked by soft hues, neutral shades, and earth tones. Denny's pastels are cheerful and welcoming, friendlier than a McDonald's edgy interior.

Blues, greens, and browns bring the outdoors in to create a refreshing "natural" atmosphere. As they absorb energy from intense reddish hues, greens, lavenders, and blues calm the nerves with "coolness."

In courtship's getting-to-know-you period, restful rooms set a mood for leisurely dining and talk. As rapport builds, couples may move to livelier "ready rooms" in taverns, lounges, and clubs, to stir passions with vibrant reds, oranges, and yellows. Notre Dame's legendary football coach Knute Rockne used a blue-colored locker room to lull opposing teams, while inciting his own players to action in more exciting red-hued quarters (Vargas, 1986). The background color scheme of a room helps or hinders in sports as well as courtship.

In restaurants, sit at window, corner, or wall tables where you are not entirely surrounded by strangers. With less distraction, your date will relate more fully to you alone.

Right Angles in Space

Whether you stand, sit, or kneel on courtship's stage, monitor your date's *angular distance*. Angular distance is the spatial orientation, measured in degrees, of another's shoulders relative to your own. As calibrated by anthropologists, angular distance is the telltale position a partner's upper body assumes relative to yours. Seeing shoulders squarely address your own calibrates as zero degrees. Zero degrees of angular distance is the friendliest position. An upper body turned sharply away to the left or right, so that all you see is one shoulder, measures ninety degrees. This angled-away posture is the snub we call the *cold shoulder*. As angular distance exceeds ninety degrees, you see more of a partner's back, suggesting all is not well.

Angular distance substitutes for linear space. The farther your partner rotates away, the farther away you feel. Conversely, when you yourself cannot politely step back from a close talker, your body instinctively twists away.

Angular distance between two people enjoying Chardonnay together reflects how they feel. Zero degrees of separation (full alignment) is a sign of mutual fondness. Facing each other and giving eye contact, with their torsos angled ninety degrees away, reflects less involvement. One partner fully aligned, with the other angled away, shows unrequited attraction—the former likes more. As sales professionals teach, never turn your upper body away from a prospect. The deflected angle shows disinterest. In courtship, too, turning away means no sale.

Faces angled away (top) show disinterest or disliking.

A side-by-side orientation (bottom) shows affection.

Orienting in Space

When you are suddenly smitten, your face, eyes, and shoulders calibrate with your partner's in zero degrees of angular distance. Your body registers love at first sight through a biological aiming instinct called the *orienting reflex*. This innate protective response provokes cognitive and emotional concerns for what is, at the moment, the most compelling thing in your sensory world. With orienting energy engaged, you cannot glance away.

STUNNED IN THE CRYSTAL ROOM

At an awards ceremony in the 1950s, a group of Hollywood's biggest stars oriented, en masse, toward one of the world's most glamorous women, Marilyn Monroe. Wearing a white satin dress, Marilyn appeared at the top of the stairs in the Crystal Room of the Beverly Hills Hotel, where the crowd awaited her arrival below. As Oscar-winner Walter Scott recalled, "It was a moment—God!—you don't forget: this girl just absolutely *stunned* that room, and just by standing at the top of the stairs. . . ." (Crown, 1987:70).

Scott used an apt word, *stun*, derived from the ancient Indo-European root *stene-*, for "thunder." In many places around the world, being suddenly smitten is likened to being struck by lightning. Like a thunderbolt, Marilyn grabbed the assembled stars' attention, filled up their senses, and momentarily became all that existed in the Crystal Room.

The orienting reflex triggers an immobility called the freeze reaction. When you come face-to-face with a stunning man or woman, you stare, your lower jaw droops, and your fingers, hands, and arms cease to move. You are fixated. The person's sheer physical presence temporarily absorbs every bit of your orienting energy. In primates a set of diagnostic signals marks the orienting reflex (Porges, 1995), making it easy to read. A thunderstruck partner greets you with lifted eyebrows, wide eyes, opened mouth, raised shoulders, a higher-pitched voice, and an Adam's-apple jump. Seeing any or all of these involuntary signs shows you've made an indelible impression. It's time to move closer together in space.

Strutting Grounds and Cruise Spots

The importance of space goes beyond interpersonal distance and the orienting reflex. Courtship is territorial in the biological sense. There are fixed property lines and defended borders. It is not accidental that we call a man's hometown his stomping ground or say that a woman rules her roost.

Territory is to courtship what a field is to football—the space in which the game is played. You can play catch without ever stepping on a football field, but serious competition takes place within the boundaries of a gridiron. By the same token, you can flirt almost anywhere, but winning a mate means pitting yourself against local rivals on the home turf. Like the courtship of fish, frogs, and ferrets, ours is nothing if not competitive.

You feel the competition and sense the territorial imperative of courtship on a Saturday night at the local teens' "cruise spot." Every city has a boulevard, plaza, mall, or downtown area where its teenagers come together in numbers to strut, flaunt, puff up, and display. In San Diego, a popular courting ground was the asphalt parking lot of Oscar's Drive-In. This frenetic nightspot drew the county's high-school youth in such numbers that police were called in nightly to close the place down. That Oscar's was a popular cruise site for twenty years shows how fixed a courting territory can be.

The teenage cruise mentality is not limited to human beings. You find the same courtship gatherings in insects, birds, and mammals in what biologists call *leks*. Derived from the Swedish word for "play," a lek is a territorial show spot. Males of a species gather in designated environs to attract females from the surrounding countryside. Only after females arrive at the mate market do courting displays and competitions begin.

Inside the lek—the same leks are used year after year—males put on dramatic eye-catching, ear-grabbing, and nose-attracting displays while the females gather to survey the field. In Central Africa, Lechwe waterbucks court in circular leks a third of a mile across. Fifty to one hundred bulls prance or stand in exaggerated, heads-held-high poses with tails wagging and penises erect. As cows enter the space, males chase one another, fight, and posture with their lyre-shaped horns. At resorts along the French Riviera, flashy men come and go in powerful, brightly colored sports cars that appeal to the opposite sex. Like waterbucks, women flock to flamboyant males who show off with the most ostentatious displays.

FIELD NOTES: LEKKING AT GOLDEN GARDENS

In spring, prairie chickens gather on display grounds to dance, strut, and attract hens in the peculiar ritual biologists call *lekking*. This form of courtship is used by many species of birds, including the sage grouse, swallow-tailed manakin, and bird of paradise as well as by some mammals, including walruses, antelopes, and bats. Inside the lek, males gather in groups to advertise their strength and availability and to showcase the special qualities that make them suitable as mates. Females enter the lek, look over the males, and make selections based on what they see and hear, and, among mammals, also smell.

In human terms, lekking resembles a job fair in which many employers assemble under one roof to meet many candidates who seek employment. It's an efficient way to do business. Among the many venues that employ spatial principles of the lek in our courtship are Club Med cruises, Mardi-gras parties, wedding receptions, salsa classes, and senior proms.

To study a human lek, I observed teenagers at Golden Gardens, a popular cruise spot on the shores of Puget Sound in Seattle. I was the only person over thirty parked in either of two rows of cars facing each other, grille to grille, across an asphalt "line of scrimmage."

With cars full of quick-eyed, hooting, beer-drinking minors lined up on either side, the cruise line was like a gauntlet. Boys rode through in gleaming vehicles hot-waxed especially for courtship, with their bodies bouncing up and down inside like chimps. A Ford pickup drove off the lot into a sandy field and spun "doughnuts," throwing up clouds of dust and divots in a show of youthful energy for all to see.

Girls in twos and threes, their faces held rigidly straight ahead, ran the gauntlet in glinting Hondas and Toyotas, also polished for the show. They returned again and again, making a circuit, but without looking sideward at the boys. Overall, it was a good show of shrieking, swaggering, high-energy courtship, teen style.

In teenage courtship, the spatial dimension is out in the open and clearly defined. So many hormones course through a young adult's veins that wooing is bound to be somewhat on the wild side. Golden Gardens officially closes at sunset, but so strong is the lekking instinct—the need to swarm increases after dark—that a patrol car shuts the park down each night with a bullhorn. After adolescence, boy-meets-girl moves to more sedate settings, to country clubs, church socials, office parties, and the like, where territory is less obvious. But discernible or not, like the invisible Coriolus force, the spatial compulsions of lekking are there to boost the assembled flock's sexual energy.

The Good Place for Courtship

According to a poll by America Online, the best courting places in the United States are Miami for the singles scene, New Orleans for "spicy encounters and secret flings," and San Francisco for ambience. Honolulu was rated best for romantic walks.

The best place to commune with someone new may not be a city but an unpeopled stretch of mountain, beach, or desert terrain. An unspoiled landscape is a place where few billboards, signposts, or symbols intrude. Information consists of natural colors, shapes, and aromas, and mostly nonhuman sounds. It's the pristine world we seek on mountaintops and island retreats, the place away from words where courtship thrives.

Mixed from blue and yellow, green combines the coolness of Alpine lakes with the happiness of sunshine. Green is the joyful color of spring leaves. Studies find that seeing green space from an apartment window reduces anxiety. Heart-rate and brain-wave research shows that nature scenes elicit a significant relaxation response. Our attraction to green vistas, sky-blue waters, and open areas between mountains and plains comes to us through the millennia from remote human ancestors. Our forebears lived in natural places and evolved positive feelings for their homeland scenes.

Courtship quickens in nature. There is less distraction from words on posters, placards, billboards, or signs. In cities, background print and broadcast media significantly divert attention. Words engulf the mind by stimulating large areas of our frontal lobes, parietal lobes, and brain stem. In urban landscapes flooded with words, couples pay less attention to faces, gestures, and postures. They relate with less involvement and immediacy than they might in the wild.

LOVERS IN THE MIST

The intoxication of natural space is clear in the peculiar courtship of primatologist Dian Fossey and anthropologist Louis Leakey, her aging mentor. In 1969 the pair went on safari from Nairobi, Kenya, through East Africa's grassy plains, where they enjoyed fine foods, vintage wines, and nights in tents with cozy beds. In his book *Woman in the Mists*, Farley Mowat (1987) writes: "Dian succumbed to the romance of star-filled nights on the sweet-smelling savanna. Leakey did more than succumb—he fell deeply, wildly in love." The surroundings must have been supernatural. Dian was thirty years younger than Louis, who was close to seventy at the time.

Ulterior Motive—Interior Design

A great deal of postadolescent courtship takes place in nightspots where men and women eat, drink, and dance, or do all three, after dark. When darkness falls, people in tribal societies huddle around campfires much as our Paleolithic ancestors did fifty thousand years ago. Nighttime brings a special feeling of intimacy. As tribe members sit and stare into burning embers, the mood becomes hushed, protective, and familiar. Human beings have long held reverent feelings for the hearth. Today, a bar-and-grill's brick-lined fireplace subliminally reassures couples who are not yet well acquainted. Wood fires calm nerves.

An underlying "fire psychology" explains why golden tints arouse happy feelings. Yellow light comes from the warm end of the color spectrum. Yellow's link with sunshine suggests airiness, brightness, and refreshment. Advertisers use the mood-altering effects of golden tints to connote achievement and modernity and to make packages look bigger. Dining in a gilt-hued room with polished brass and glowing gaslights establishes warmth that flows from the space outward, to the people within.

Fireplace or not, nightspots offer definite advantages. Upon entering a darkened area we reflexively quiet and slow our pace. A reverent mood comes upon us when we step into a dimly lit cathedral. In courtship, subdued lighting makes a roomful of strangers easier to bear. They seem spatially farther away and, psychologically, further removed. Meanwhile, you move closer to your date. As personal space shrinks in the darkened setting, faces loom nearer. Intimacy increases with decreases in light.

Candlelight from a crystal globe on the table makes your face look younger and softer than it looks in sunlight. The dancing flame casts a hypnotic spell that makes eye contact easier. You spend more time watching facial cues for telltale signs of affection.

To be on the same wavelength in courtship, take your date to a themed space. As a musical theme's principal melody unites you in song, a themed interior's story line unites you in space. The theme concept was born in the 1950s in California on Disneyland's Main Street. Disney created a Victorian space with thematically unified architecture. Nothing upsets the Gay Nineties motif. You see no billboards or flashing neon signs on Main Street. Buildings are scaled smaller than real life to make you feel larger than life. Everything on Main Street reassures, with nothing out of place to jar your senses. The theme draws you into a sheltered space where all, seemingly, is well.

For a romantic dining experience, visit Harrah's Range Steakhouse, a restaurant with a Western theme. In Harrah's canyon setting you feel as if you are cooking together "out on the range." Accenting colors and downlights create an interior with the look and feel of a canyon at sunset. Booths are partitioned with vertically ascending branches and tree limbs illuminated by the glow of nearby "campfires." The restaurant's grill is framed by a rock-wall mural embedded with neon lights to create the effect of a cascading stream.

Immersed in Harrah's nonverbal narrative, you share a canyon-at-sunset experience that brings you closer. Moods harmonize under the influence of thematic design features. Like other theme spaces, Harrah's emits signals reminiscent of the comforting rural past. In an Old West or Australian Outback interior, you step back out of the disturbing present into the good old days. Away from pressing concerns here and now, courtship is easy.

THE MORE YOU know about spatial communication, the easier courtship becomes. From where you sit, stand, speak, or posture in a room to the color scheme, lighting, and décor of the room itself, spatial cues powerfully affect your demeanor and presentation of self. In the next chapter, I turn from the visible world of spaces, places, and interiors to the invisible world of chemical cues, smell, and taste.

11. CHEMICAL CUES

The meeting of two personalities is like the
contact of two chemical substances: if there is any
reaction, both are transformed.

—CARL JUNG

ANY OF COURTSHIP'S most powerful signals are unheard, untouched, and unseen. They are the chemical attractors, and their medium is the molecule. Operating chiefly through unconscious channels, these invisible aromas, tastes, steroids, sterols, and hormones strongly shape our feelings about each other and about the physical settings in which we meet.

Men and women find something strangely appealing and sexy, for example, about the smell of a new car's interior. Many couples find that new-car aroma accelerates the "getting to know you" process. This is not surprising, because a motor vehicle's passenger compartment houses products made of leather, rubber, plastic, and vinyl. The molecular ingredients of these materials are chemical analogs of natural plant resins, animal esters, and human sexual steroids (Stoddart, 1990). We find the aromatic structure of such natural compounds—and of their automotive counterparts—peculiarly enticing.

Vinyl contains the chemical compound ethylene (C_2H_4), which resembles the fragrant sterols of incense and the male steroid testosterone ($C_{19}H_{28}O_2$). So captivating to the nose are such chemical emanations that International Flavors and Fragrances of New York has developed a product called New Car Smell. To enliven a used car's sex appeal we simply spray the aphrodisiacal fluid into the vehicle from an aerosol can.

Scent of a Woman, Smell of a Man

Like New Car Smell, sexual steroids have an aromatic allure. The female hormone estrogen gives off a mildly sweaty, animallike scent. Many find estrogen's aroma bland or neutral, whereas some find it slightly unpleasant. Testosterone has much the same sweaty, animalistic smell, with overtones of urine, musk, and goat.

Whether you judge sexual steroids as neutral, pleasing, or unpleasing to the nose, even if you can't smell them at all, they definitely register in your brain's hypothalamus. The hypothalamus is a tiny part of the forebrain in charge of primitive sexual urges and instincts. A PET-scan study by Ivanka Savic and his colleagues at Stockholm's Huddinge University Hospital found that estrogenlike compounds affect sexually responsive parts of a man's hypothalamus (the *paraventricular* and *dorsomedial nuclei*) but not those of a woman (Savic et al., 2001). Vice versa, testosteronelike substances stimulate sexually responsive parts of a woman's hypothalamus (the *preoptic* and *ventromedial nuclei*) but not those of a man. Clearly, we respond to each other's sexual steroids by gender, apart from conscious awareness.

> For men, the smell of estrogen increases blood flow to the hypothalamus, a thumbnail-size structure deep in the forebrain. For women, the smell of testosterone does the same.

Where do steroid scents come from? Your strongest sexual aromas are emitted by specialized scent glands in your underarms called *apocrine glands*. After bathing, you should wear an unscented deodorant, applied lightly, to ensure that apocrine traces register in your partner's brain. With some testing you will find a balance between over- and underdeodorizing for the right subliminal effect.

Steve, thirty-five, a computer programmer who is reluctantly single, wears too much deodorant. This is a common mistake of men. Assuming they smell bad, men overdeodorize to extinguish every trace of apocrine smell. But in Steve's case his roll-on, not his body odor, is the fragrance that offends. Unknown to him, the scent saturates his work cubicle and the cubicles around him. At parties women avoid him and complain that that "Steve smell" rubs off when he hugs them good-bye. Around the office Steve is known as the sweet guy with the sour smell. To women his message is fatal: "You don't smell right; I'm not dating you."

On a conscious level, women are five times more sensitive to musky aromas than men are. As a man, you should emit at most only a hint of underarm smell. As a woman—because half of all men are oblivious to musky scents—you may send "louder" apocrine messages to accent your perfumes with an untamed animal glow. A woman is most sensitive to a man's apocrine at the midpoint of her menstrual cycle as ovulation takes place. His chemical message should be subtle, enough to address her hypothalamus without offending her nose.

Aroma Cues Lend Presence

The olfactory sense evolved as an early warning system to detect predators, food, and mates from a distance. As warning, eating, and mating signs, aroma cues are taken very seriously by the brain. Smell is a volatile, "thin-skinned" sense because scent receptors lie on the bodily surface itself, on the nasal cavity's *olfactory epithelium*, rather than beneath layers of skin, as in touch. Few changes have been made in aroma receptors since the time of the jawless fishes 500 million years ago, making smell our most conservative, compelling, and trusted sense. When we smell smoke, we absolutely "know" there is fire.

Smell is our oldest nonverbal channel. Though the primate sense of smell is weaker than that of most mammals, we are still able to recognize some ten thousand natural and manufactured scents. Many of these can alter our sexual desires, feelings, and moods.

S perm cells have a chemical sensor that causes them to swim toward the scent of a female's egg.

Aroma cues can be traced far back in time to the chemical messages sent and received by simple creatures who courted mates in primordial seas. Today, in our own courtship, understanding the biology of smell provides powerful leverage. In the physical closeness of dance, the body's natural aromas should not be completely masked or washed away. As we have seen, this is true even for our most maligned scent, apocrine odor. Body odor, or BO, is a pungent smell produced by dense concentrations of apocrine glands in the underarms and by lesser concentrations in the face, scalp, ears, eyelids, navel, and genital area. Too much body odor is offensive, but in trace amounts it sends a warm, emotionally arousing message.

Before courtship, the surface of a newborn's skin is covered with apocrine glands that give off an identifiable "baby smell." These are eventually replaced by mature scent glands in the underarms, chest, and groin area. Thick hairs in these regions broadcast apocrine scent by increasing the surface area from which it wicks. Due to their attracting role in courtship, human underarms have the largest scent glands of any primate.

Controlled by sympathetic nerves of the fight-or-flight response, apocrine glands discharge a thick, milky substance in response to emotion. In courtship, scent is released as apocrine undergoes bacterial decomposition to produce androstenone and odorous fatty acids which announce our sexual moods. These glandular messages of arousal broadcast below the radar screen of awareness. They are picked up subconsciously by the partner's *rhinencephalon*. The rhinen-cephalon, or "nose brain," is a primitive part of the cerebrum which, like our hypothalamus, mediates feeding and sexual behavior.

Apocrine traces too tiny to register in consciousness can measurably affect your date's blood pressure, respiration, and heart rate. Many deodorants, colognes, and perfumes contain scents designed, like apocrine odor itself, to mimic the musky aromas of our own sexual steroids.

Where Sexual Chemistry Gallops

Without knowing why, men and women find each other more attractive at the county fair. In late summer and early fall, county fairs are hot, noisy, and crowded—and bursting with sexually attractive chemical cues. Hay, sage, mesquite smoke, sawdust, maple syrup, dill weed, and horse sweat release aromatic plant sterols and animal steroids into the open air.

Also airborne is the incense of kettle corn, Belgian waffles, and curly fries. At the fair, your hypothalamus responds to chemical cues emitted by foods in tandem with cues that announce sexuality. The signals synergistically combine to make you feel, as one young woman puts it, "like getting married and having kids immediately." Romantic ambience fades as you leave the fairground, but in the sense-surround of the fair itself, with love molecules in the air, you feel like holding hands at the least. You feel it, your date feels it, the cowboys and the horses feel it. Chemistry is happening in every cubic inch of air.

The Best Kisses Are Scented

Another seductive fragrance—detectable while dancing cheek to cheek—is a tallowlike substance called *sebum*. Each of your body's sixty-five hair follicles per square inch gives off a mildly pleasant, adultlike scent as sebum is secreted into the hair shaft by mammalian *sebaceous glands*. Human beings have significantly more sebaceous glands than other mammals. They are larger in men than in women. At adolescence, the output of sebaceous glands triples to convince a partner's nose that you are sexually mature.

With most sebum, the oiliest parts of the body are your eyelids, nose, and forehead. You also have sebaceous glands in the skin lining your mouth and lips—especially in your upper lip where dry and moist tissues meet—to enhance the scent of a kiss. Sebum evolved as a waterproofing substance to protect fur from becoming overly wet. Today, sebum plays a role in establishing your unique "signature" scent. Like French wines, no two bodies smell exactly alike. When kissing is imminent, avoid heavy petroleum-based lip products, high-shine lip gloss, and overly thick "wet" lipsticks. Sebum's naturally odorous linoleic, oleic, and palmitic acids form a distinctive bouquet that is better left uncovered.

A Fruity-Floral Fragrance Says, "Approach Me"

The best perfumes for women release aromas of flowers and fruit. Our primate ancestors were tree-climbing fruit eaters, and we have a strong appetite for the sweetness of fruit today. Apple, apricot, litchi, black currant, mandarin, plum, or peach fragrances in your perfume— along with the floral smell of lily, orchid, orange blossom, or rose— combine to arouse passion. Your date's primeval nose brain oversees feeding as well as sexual appetites. Biologically, your fruity fragrance seems to say "I am edible; you may approach."

Arpège is a classic floral perfume. Created in 1927 by Jeanne Lanvin, it is still a world bestseller. Arpège strategically bypasses thinking parts of your partner's neocortex and speaks directly to emotion centers of his mammalian brain. Combining fruity rose, jasmine, orange blossom, and sixty natural oils and extracts, Arpège has a potent effect on the male nose. The name itself, derived from the Italian word *arpeggio*, a musical term for playing the tones of a chord in quick succession rather than simultaneously, reflects the perfume's stratigraphic layers of smell.

The Best Perfumes Are Layered

Superior women's fragrances have three layered odor groups called *notes*. Arpège's top note, rose, registers first; its middle note, jasmine, provides body; and its base note, musk, gives warmth, texture, and staying power (Stoddart, 1990). Initially your date detects the floral aromas of the top and middle notes, which smell temptingly sweet. Then the sexually stimulating aroma of animal musk hits pleasure centers of his brain. Fragrance designer Ann Gottlieb reports that men find fruitiness—especially combined with the sweet and warm aroma of vanilla or amber—"very, very sexy indeed."

A man's nose quickly habituates to the smell of your perfume. After a few moments his primary olfactory cortex tunes out your scent. For perfume to cast its spell, periodically leave your partner and return to give your fragrance a chance to refresh and renew. If your date is a smoker, has allergies, lives in a smoggy metropolis, or works in a chemical plant, his nose is less liable to pick up your aromas. For a signature scent, mix your favorite floral aromas with essential oils of your choosing, such as cinnamon, coriander, and vanilla.

A PERFUME TO MAKE YOU "THINNER"

A decade-long study suggests that you seem slimmer by wearing combined floral and spicy perfumes. Directed by neurologist Alan Hirsch of the Smell & Taste Treatment and Research Foundation in Chicago, the study found that men perceived women who wore spicy-floral fragrances to be an average twelve pounds lighter.

"It acts as the olfactory equivalent to vertical lines," Hirsch remarked, alluding to the slimming effect of a dress's vertical stripes. Presented at the 2003 meeting of the Association for Chemoreception Sciences, Hirsch's study determined that the slimming effect worked only with spicy-floral scents. Other scents, sprays, and perfumes did not produce the illusion.

Your Aftershave Should Whisper

The best cologne for a man is herbal or spicy rather than sweet. Throughout the world women smell sweet and fruity in courtship while men smell "woodsy." Wearing a sandalwood aftershave says, "I am here," and calls subliminal attention to the wearer's testosterone level. Experiments show that women compare male-steroid aromas to the smell of sandalwood, cedar, and balsam (Stoddart, 1990). But since the aroma of pungent herbs and spices is more piercing than the scent of fruits and flowers, and since a woman's nose is more sensitive than a man's, he should wear cologne lightly. A penetrating aroma can make him seem too woodsy—and too close—too soon.

Actually, a man is better off in the early stages of courtship wearing no fragrance at all. Many colognes, lotions, and aftershaves assault the female nose. Smell, more than any other sense, evokes strong feelings of approach—or avoidance. Many women have negative reactions to masculine-scented products generally, deeming them too "forward." On a date, women prefer natural to synthetic scents.

Fragrance is critical in courtship, because our emotional brain is closely tied to the sense of smell. Since the primary olfactory cortex projects to the amygdala, strong feelings are aroused. Our almond-size amygdala, an arousal center that originated millions of years ago in the earliest fishes, receives fibers directly from the olfactory bulb. This means that aroma cues emitted from scent glands, perfumes, and powders trigger emotions in a direct and immediate way (Nauta and Feirtag, 1979). Neurologist Alan Hirsch may be right in recommending that men wear baby powder to arouse a woman's maternal-caring instincts.

Food Sharing and Lovemaking Are Linked

Like the sense of smell, the chemical sense of taste evokes potent feelings in courtship. Taste evolved more than 500 million years ago as a chemical means for prevertebrate ancestors to detect food. Today, in accord with a worldwide rite of passage in courtship, we share food before we make love.

Through combinations of aroma and taste in romantic cuisines, we experience a seductive force called *flavor*. Flavor emanates from the likes of Tuscan olive oils, Tasmanian duck, and truffles. The English word *flavor* evolved from the Indo-European root *bhlo-*, which means "blow up" or "blast." Some lexicographers find an allusion to sexual swelling in the ancient root.

Around the globe, the best courting recipes feature meat. We crave meaty tastes because our hunger for flesh is older than our more recently acquired primate taste for fruits, nuts, and berries. In prehistoric times the brain's amygdala played a role in the pursuit, handling, and killing of game. It also stimulated the release of digestive juices in preparation for eating the kill (Carlson, 1986). Today, as in the past, hidden aggressiveness in the meat eater's code makes a spicy meatball or broiled steak more exciting on dinner dates than a leaf salad or bowl of fruit.

Lively Foods Enliven Courtship

For a romantic meal, awaken your partner's palate with *trigeminal taste*. The trigeminal sense is a recently discovered, third chemical sensor that works alongside ordinary taste and smell. Named for the brain's trigeminal nerve (cranial V), it is part of our oral cavity's tactile sense. Most of us enjoy the trigeminal pungency of black pepper or piperine, red chili pepper or capsaicin, mustard, and horseradish. A pungent spice awakens courtship much as it enlivens a dip or sauce.

Along with hot, our trigeminal sense favors cool spices, such as mint or menthol, and enjoys the chemically sharp taste of alcohol in tequila, bourbon, and rum. Courtship is enhanced not only by the intoxicating effect of alcohol itself but also by its bite. The trigeminal sense evolved as an early warning system for pain, to protect the tongue and oral cavity from potentially toxic substances. Seasonings such as parsley, sage, rosemary, and thyme add zest to food. Since our senses generalize what we experience, an excited palate makes a partner more exciting to be with.

Many of the world's romantic cuisines originated in Italy. With melted mozzarella, tomato sauce, basil, and roasted garlic, pizza makes a lively choice today. Certain Italian tastes are esteemed for stimulating the front and the back of the throat at the same time. Made from earlier harvested green olives, Tuscan oils leave a peppery flavor in the pharynx. The mildly hot taste of Tuscan oils is sensed as a tactile irritant by the same trigeminal nerves that enjoy carbonated colas and the astringence of Chianti. A romantic meal should be nothing if not flavorful and, through the trigeminal sense, also arousing.

What gives trigeminal taste its sex appeal? Some propose that capsaicin in hot peppers releases opiumlike substances that address the brain as pleasure cues. Capsaicin is one of thousands of what botanists call "secondary products," active ingredients found in herbs and spices. Secondary products, such as cyanogenic compounds and insect-repelling hormones, evolved to defend plants against bugs, snails, and other leaf-eating pests. Their message is: "Do not eat me!" The secondary products our trigeminal sense tastes warn that a leaf, stem, seed, or fruit is dangerous to swallow. In small amounts, their warning messages put our senses on heightened alert with subliminal tastes of danger. As we'll soon see in the Capilano Canyon study, danger is a heady theme in courtship.

Chocolate Sex Appeal

The optimal dessert for courting couples is chocolate. Chemically, chocolate combines the sweetness of sugar—which has a calming effect on infants, reducing their reactions to pain (Blass, 1992)—with an amphetamine-like molecule, *phenylethylamine* or PEA, and the amino acid *tryptophan*. These substances release mood-enhancing chemicals into the brain.

Chocolate's tryptophan ($C_{11}H_{12}N_2O_2$) is a precursor molecule that transforms into the neurotransmitter *serotonin* ($C_{10}H_{12}N_2O$). Drugs like Prozac, Zoloft, and Paxil keep higher levels of the natural, mood-elevating chemical in the brain. Serotonin makes you feel good about life and, in courtship, good about each other. After eating a chocolate bar, tryptophan circulates through the bloodstream into the cerebrum across the blood-brain barrier. There, as serotonin, it constricts blood vessels and stimulates smooth muscles of the digestive system. Serotonin has a combined mood-elevating, tranquilizing effect that makes "getting to know you" easy.

Chocolate's PEA is a chemical compound the body manufactures when we fall in love. The presence of PEA's "love molecule" could explain why the Aztecs associated chocolate with fertility. Tests show that only a small amount of PEA actually gets through to the brain after we consume a chocolate bar. But the body itself produces psychoactive amounts of the neurotransmitter when we feel sexually aroused. PEA plays a role in a complex of messaging molecules that release dopamine into the brain's pleasure pathway. In courtship, researchers claim, PEA's euphoric effects may be triggered by a single hug, a touch of the hand, or love at first sight.

In the mid-1990s, Monash University scientists Peter Godfrey, Lynette Hatherley, and Ron Brown announced the discovery of PEA's chemical structure. For the first few years of a relationship, says biologist Robert Friar of Ferris State University, PEA makes us less aware of a new love's faults. So energizing are its amphetamine-like properties, Friar notes, that a romantic mood can be detected in breathlessness, sweaty palms, throbbing carotid arteries, flushed cheeks, and weak knees.

These are the same physical symptoms—shaking, blushing, weakness, and stammering—that psychologist Dorothy Tennov found in a survey of four hundred people she had asked to explain what being in love actually "feels like" (Tennov, 1979). In *The Chemistry of Love* (1983), psychiatrist Michael Liebowitz claimed that PEA stimulates boundless energy and yields symptoms of temporary insanity. Giddiness may be the definitive sign of a positive chemical reaction in courtship.

The Question of Aphrodisiacs

Chocolate and PEA lead to a perennial polemic: aphrodisiacs. Overall, scientists disagree as to whether aphrodisiacs work or even exist. Yet many foods traditionally considered arousing do, in fact, inspire chemical responses in the body. An example is the truffle, a homely mushroom considered aphrodisiacal since the time of Socrates. Scientists have found that the musky, oddly shaped fungus contains high levels of a hormone related to masculine testosterone called *androsterone*.

A frequently used mood enhancer in courtship is the common cocktail. After two drinks your companion feels less inhibited, more relaxed, and emotionally closer to you. By any definition, ethyl alcohol (C_2H_5OH) is an aphrodisiac. Alcohol eases stranger anxiety and alleviates emotions of the fight-or-flight response. Cocktails alter the transmission of messages between nerve cells in your own and in your partner's brain.

Alcohol stimulates the release of dopamine into pleasure centers of both brains. Temporarily, drinking together makes you feel good together. You generalize the warm glow of brandy to the affection felt for each other. Chemically induced good feelings become "good vibrations." Alcohol has been a player in courtship since Mesopotamian times. The Greeks courted in Dionysian drinking rituals. Romans romanced in bacchanalia. Students party with pizza, beer, and wine today.

Aphrodisiacal Signals

"Love looks not with the eyes, but with the mind," Shakespeare wrote in *A Midsummer-Night's Dream*. He may have had aphrodisiacs on his own mind. Whether their effects on libido are physiological, psychological, or psychiatric, aphrodisiacs send messages which, for believers, inspire chemical reactions that measurably heighten arousal:

- For centuries in the East, the aroma of musk has been prized as an aphrodisiac. Though animal musk has been used in perfumes for fifty-five hundred years, today it has been replaced by less potent synthetics.
- Sexually suggestive shapes of asparagus, artichokes, avocados, and bananas have been thought to stimulate desire. Their textures, flavors, and aromas bespeak sexuality as well.
- Oysters mimic the look, feel, and aroma of female genitalia. Those who eat them liken the experience to oral sex.
- Abundant seeds of pomegranates and tomatoes symbolize fertility. They have aphrodisiacal properties in some cultures.
- Celery contains androsterone, a male hormone women find sexually stimulating.
- Gingko nuts reputedly improve libido.
- Ancient Greeks believed orchid roots were aphrodisiacs.
- Native Americans used wood betony and American lousewort as aphrodisiacs, boiling the leaves and stems to make a pot herb.

Addiction to Love

Chemical feelings of arousal in courtship are nonspecific. Pleasure is the same at the molecular level whether due to sex, drugs, rock 'n' roll, or chocolate. As University of Minnesota researcher Marilyn Carroll points out, the same neurochemicals mediate food, alcohol, and drug experiences. In courtship, sexual arousal, infatuation, and falling in love happen as chemically encoded messages engage the brain's half-billion-year-old pleasure pathway. The hub of this primordial pathway is an area in the front of the brain called the *nucleus accumbens*. Some think it causes our species' peculiar addiction to love.

Research high above rushing waters in the mountains of British Columbia, a project known as the Capilano Canyon Suspension Bridge Study, shows how fear—amplified by the hormone *adrenaline* ($C_9H_{13}NO_3$)—heightens sexual attraction between complete strangers.

The Capilano findings have an immediate application in courtship. You stand a better chance of falling in love when you share an emotionally arousing date together. Though dinner and a movie has its charm, scuba diving, off-roading, or riding roller-coasters are more likely to arouse passions needed for chemical bonding to take place.

In the Capilano study, an attractive woman approached and spoke to thirty-four men, all of whom were strangers ranging in age from eighteen to thirty-five. One by one, she met and talked with each of the men. Half the unsuspecting partners were on the swaying suspension bridge. Perilously high above the gorge, they were "adrenaline aroused." The other half she met were on firm ground, near but not actually on the bridge itself. They, the study's control group, were "not aroused." Subsequently each man was asked to write about the good-looking stranger. Adrenaline-aroused men included significantly more sexual imagery in stories than the non-aroused controls. Moreover, adrenaline-charged males were more likely to make contact with the woman later by phone.

From his observations at Capilano Canyon, social psychologist Arthur Aron concluded that arousal due to fear had been mistaken for arousal due to sexual attraction (Dutton and Aron, 1974). In courtship, since chemically induced feelings of fear and arousal are nonspecific, they are easily confused. Arousal from danger—triggering the release of adrenaline into the bloodstream—feels like arousal from infatuation. Adrenal hormones increase heart rate, blood pressure, blood sugar, and metabolism in both situations.

The chemical bond between sex and danger was tested in New York at the beginning of the twenty-first century. In a *Time* magazine article on "Dating After Doomsday," Manhattan couples explained how much easier it had been to start a conversation with a total stranger right after the September 11, 2001, toppling of the World Trade Center (Tyrangiel, 2002). "I was struck by how easily we could just jump into a conversation," a woman said. Names given the phenomenon at the time—"apocalypse sex" and "disaster tryst"—reflect powerful emotions. Like the emotions felt on Capilano Bridge, they greatly accelerated courtship. As a man who shared an intimate evening with a woman he met on a New York subway remarked, "Pretty much all we talked about was the World Trade Center and how glad we were to be alive."

For a more perfect union, plan your next outing with adrenaline in mind. Have a dating adventure. Go mountain biking, hike the Grand Canyon, or parasail together. The thrill of gravity-defying activities arouses passion and keeps love alive. Aron's findings benefit established couples who continue to have challenging exploits together. Chemical love signals can strengthen the pair bond throughout life.

Cuddle Compound

The pleasure you feel "just being near" is reinforced by the messaging molecule *oxytocin* ($C_{43}H_{66}N_{12}O_{12}S_2$). As relationships mature, the pituitary hormone "oxy" sends chemical messages to pleasure pathways of your, and your partner's, brain. Oxytocin causes you to crave each other as you crave addictive comfort foods. Oxytocin's chemical output increases in the teen years, prompting adolescent crushes. In adults oxy brings drowsiness after lovemaking. Neurobiologist Sue Carter from the University of Illinois at Chicago believes oxytocin is at the "very central core" of our sexual communication (Rodgers, 2001:260). For Quentin Pittman of the University of Calgary's Neuroscience Research Group, oxytocin could explain why we long for just one partner at a time.

Chemical Magnetism

Courtship's most powerful molecules may be *pheromones*. In many animal species, females release aphrodisiacal fragrances to lure mates as their eggs mature. An erotic nose, the *vomeronasal organ*, or VNO, has been discovered in mammals. The VNO detects pheromones through receptors other than those for ordinary smell. Some scientists think that we, too, may attract directly through hormonal compounds released from our breath, saliva, and sweat, but the existence of a human pheromone is controversial as is evidence for a human VNO.

Isolated in the mid-1950s, the first scientifically identified pheromone came from an insect, the silkworm moth. The female's sexually attractive compound caused male moths to move their wings wildly in a "flutter dance." That they fluttered purely on chemical command is central to the definition of the term. A pheromone triggers involuntary actions.

Provocative evidence for pheromones comes from studies showing that airborne cues emitted by women living together in dorms affect the timing of each other's menstrual cycle (Stern and McClintock, 1998). Conclusive evidence for a sexually attractive pheromone, however, has yet to be found in humans. In his prestigious January 1, 2001, "Annual Review of Psychology" article evaluating research on smell, Richard L. Doty concluded that our brain simply lacks the necessary neuronal components to pick up a pheromone's scented message.

There is little doubt that chemistry boosts your sexual magnetism.

"I'm coming to see you," Napoleon wrote his girlfriend. "Don't wash." The perfect "lotus woman," the *Kama Sutra* teaches, emits an attracting odor of musk. In tribal societies, lovers exchange scent-laden garments to keep each other always in mind. Italian adventurer Giovanni Casanova described an intimate, balsamlike aroma emanating from his lovers' bedrooms. Minuscule molecules say more than a little in courtship.

Psychoactive chemical signals in cars, deodorants, perfumes, food, drink, and seasonings—in tandem with chemical cues emitted by your own body—play an indispensable role in the courtship of our species. There is little doubt that chemistry boosts sexual magnetism.

12. STAYING TOGETHER—
NONVERBAL CUES
THAT BIND

To be loved, be lovable.
—OVID (*ARS AMATORIA*)

FTER THOUSANDS OF love signals sent, a life-altering message is received: "I choose you!" Giving yourself to another puts you on an emotionally higher plain on which you transform as a loving pair. Verbally, the word *I* takes a backseat to the word *we*. Nonverbally, the world seems a better place, livelier, friendlier, brighter, full of fun. You laugh, gaze into each other's eyes, and walk with a spring in your step.

At first, infatuation may make you stammer, shake, blush, and go weak in the knees. According to psychologist Dorothy Tennov, author of *Love and Limerence: The Experience of Being in Love,* intense affection brings on a buoyancy like walking on air, an intoxication when your partner is near, and a pain at the front of your chest when your partner is away.

Predictably, infatuation is temporary. "Things are always best in their beginning," Pascal wrote, and the giddy feeling of "being in love" doesn't last forever. Tennov maintains that the average length of a romantic obsession is two years. After courtship brings you physically, emotionally, and passionately together, you face a dilemma. Should you simply enjoy your months of passionate love and then seek someone new? Or, should you stay together and pursue the more mature relationship known as *companionate love?*

Passionate vs. Companionate Love

Psychologist Elaine Hatfield thinks we experience two kinds of love in a lifetime, *passionate* and *companionate* love. Passionate, also called romantic, love is a combination of high sexual desire, emotional elation, and profound longing for another person. It can last anywhere from six to thirty months, and for this relatively short period of time we feel swept off our feet.

A nonverbal sign of passionate love is the *head-contact* gesture. Touching a partner's head with a hand or with one's own head is a widespread signal of physical attraction. "Hand-to-head contacts," Desmond Morris writes, "are four times as common between young lovers as between older married couples," and head-to-head contacts are twice as likely between new lovers as between established pairs (Morris, 1983:141).

Head-to-head contact is a nonverbal sign of passionate love. Momentary eye closure is common when romantic feeling runs high.

Couples send fewer passionate love signals after Phase Five. Having closed the physical gap, they relax in each other's company as a "mated pair." Successful couples con-

tinue to exchange companionate love signals. Struggling couples merely talk.

Companionate, also known as affectionate, love, is less physically passionate but stable and longer lasting. It includes deep feelings of attachment, loyalty, and familiarity developed over time. Under its spell,
you like and feel like caring for each other. Companionate love is as
strong as passionate love but sexually less intense.

A nonverbal sign of companionate love is the *shoulder embrace*.
More often than new lovers, Morris claims, established couples touch
each other's shoulders and upper arms with their fingertips and
opened palms. Though less intimate than "putting your heads together," the shoulder embrace shows caring, liking, and loving with a
simple touch of the hands.

In happy relationships, nonverbal communication continues as
passionate love evolves into companionate love. Serotonin levels rise,
and at a given point the security of companionship supersedes the
thrill of passion. Sociologist David Popenoe has found that men and
women in companionate relationships live longer, happier, healthier
lives.

Of course, not all couples reach the companionate plateau.
Though 95 percent of Americans marry, half divorce, and the most
common reason for seeking professional help is a relationship problem (Fincham et al., 1993). Given these challenges, you might ask if
there's a fundamental problem with our freewheeling style of
courtship. Should we marry for love or should we leave courting to
matchmakers as millions in India, China, and Japan do and opt for an
arranged marriage instead?

The answer is simple: seek love. Anthropologists have found that
arranged marriages face the same challenges as unions based on personal choice. In the former, couples still must court before making
love and must learn to like—and to love—each other enough for

companionate bonds to emerge. The key to success in free-form courtship is being a careful observer. As you look for passionate-love signals with one eye, watch for companionate signs with the other.

Why do relationships end? Women complain they receive too few affectionate cues. Men complain about a partner's whining tone of voice (Fincham et al., 1993).

Body Language with Strangers Is Key

Companionate love is less about sex than about taking care. As a man, you'll find evidence of your date's caring aptitude in the body language she uses with strangers. In a supermarket, does she lift her eyebrows, tilt her head, and speak in a higher-pitched voice with clerks? These signals reveal an empathic personality conducive to a long-term relationship. Or does she avoid eye contact, lower her eyebrows, and speak in a curt, impatient, or indifferent voice? The way she treats people in everyday life—in a friendly, unfriendly, or blasé manner—shows how you could be treated when passions subside.

Watch your partner's body language with strangers to see how he or she may deal with you later on.

If a waiter sets the wrong entrée in front of your date, does he narrow his eyes, curl his upper lip, and shake his head in annoyance? These and other micromomentary cues, like slitted eyes and vertical wrinkles above the nose, which can last less than a second, telegraph a mood shift. That his facial muscles contract on impulse shows he cares less about the server than about himself. The fleeting expression of anger—which comes and goes in a flash—is a cautionary sign. On his best behavior with you now, the flare-up shows he could lose his temper with you later on.

In love's passionate stage you naturally focus on what your partner's body says to you and miss, or choose to ignore, signs addressed to others. "My husband has so much anger and seems to blame me much of the time," a young wife writes. "He loses his temper at least once a day and yells at me." Surely, she saw him target others with outbursts before they married. That we overlook signs of hotheadedness in courtship's passionate stage is one reason marital misery and divorce rates are high.

BODY LANGUAGE PREDICTS MARITAL SUCCESS

In a twenty-year study of more than six hundred married couples, nonverbal signs of anger, harshness, and hostility were factored into a mathematical formula to predict which marriages would likely fail within six to sixteen years. Researchers watched as husbands and wives interacted, then coded verbal and nonverbal behavior to gauge the likelihood of marital success or failure. The study, by John Gottman of the Relationship Institute and the University of Washington, found that nonverbal displays of humor, friendliness, and affection were strong predictors of success.

Anger tops the list of negative emotions that work against companionate love. A mammalian elaboration of older vertebrate patterns for aggression and physical combat, anger clearly shows in demeanor. Hands ball into fists, lips compress, nostrils flare. Muscles around the eyebrows contract in frowning. *Corrugator supercilii* blended with *occipitofrontalis* and *orbicularis oculi* draw the brows downward and create vertical furrows above the nose. Gut-reactive masseter muscles tense the lower jaw for biting.

An angry voice is louder and deeper in pitch. "The more threatened or aggressive an animal becomes," science journalist Janet Hopson writes, "the lower and harsher its voice turns—thus, the bigger it seems" (Hopson, 1980:83). Loud volume makes the body loom "larger" and more threatening. Expressed with the same nonverbal signs in every culture, anger is never a good sign in courtship.

Signs of deception are disturbing as well. Is your partner sometimes untruthful with others? Lying sabotages companionate love by destroying trust. Deception is a common problem in millions of marriages because, thanks to a peculiar fact of human biology, deceiving is easy. Deception is common in our closest primate relatives, the monkeys and apes. Chimpanzees, who share 99 percent of our DNA, are truly gifted deceivers. Zoologist Frans de Waal tells the story of Luit, an adult male, who pressed his lips together with his hand to hide the submissive fear grin he had given his rival, Nikki (Waal, 1982). Luit, like many humans, tried to mask his inner feelings with a deceptive cue.

In courtship, deception is often covered up with anger. "For nearly a month," a thirty-year-old man writes, "my girlfriend has been e-mailing a guy from high school she found on her class website. They carry on serious e-mail, but whenever I ask about it she gets really upset with me." Her anger is a deceptive ploy. Partners make fists, raise their voices, and glare to camouflage signs of lying. In this case, yelling is a smoke screen to keep her boyfriend from learning of the e-mail affair. Her anger display does not bode well for a long-term relationship.

The top four nonverbal signs of deception are:

1. A lower rate of head nodding.
2. Increased eye blinking.
3. Greater use of self-touching gestures, especially contact between the fingertips and lips or nose.
4. Using fewer hand gestures while speaking.

Deceptive partners telegraph anxiety with evasive eye movements, rapid eyeblinks, and fidgeting digits. Unconvinced by their own words, they withhold gestures normally used to emphasize speaking points. Instead of gesticulating, hands clasp tightly together and fingers entwine. Guilt and uncertainty show as eyeballs rotate downward, unable to meet your gaze. Higher stress requires more oxygen, and a visible "switch point" is reached as breathing shifts from the nose to the mouth.

Nonverbal signs of deception and anger clearly show a relationship is in trouble. A more insidious sign is when couples no longer find time to touch. When the loving feeling goes, the next thing to go is touching:

I've been married for eight years to my college sweetheart. We have two young children, a girl and a boy. Last night after dinner my husband was unusually quiet in the family room. I asked him what's wrong, and without any warning he told me he didn't love me anymore and wanted a divorce. I was petrified and speechless. For years we've had a little ritual where we say "I love you" at least once everyday. We hardly touch anymore, but since we put our love in words, I thought we were okay. This morning he told me again that he doesn't love me.

Companionate Love Signals

NONSEXUAL TOUCHING. More immediate and far more powerful than words, touching, hugging, and hand-holding are essential signs to reassure that you care. Neurologically, words are processed in higher levels of cerebral cortex before affective content registers in emotional centers below. Touch cues, on the other hand, go directly to emotion centers before registering in the cerebral cortex. Regular touching has a healing effect that keeps couples together through life's daily stresses. Touching not only shows you care but also increases the flow of pleasure-producing endorphins released into the nervous system.

Hug your partner twice a day to care for, comfort, and show your love. If seeing is believing, touching is knowing "for sure."

A way to reconnect in the tactile mode is with the "twenty-second kiss." Prescribed by marriage counselors as a homework assignment, couples set aside a time to kiss for twenty seconds each day. Lengthy labile contact raises the male's testosterone level as it stimulates feelings of attachment and closeness in the female. Couples also connect through regular shoulder, hand, and foot massages. Linked to emotionally sensitive nerves, lips, shoulders, hands, and feet feel emotionally stimulated when touched.

A LOVING VOICE. To hear a loving voice, speak in loving tones. Research by Stanford Gregory and Stephen Webster of Kent State University reveals that couples unconsciously adapt to each other's voice tones. Speak softly, they advise, to hear softness back. Talk in annoyed, demanding, sarcastic tones and hear these tones back. Gregory and Webster, who study *communication accommodation theory*, report that you can control the tenor of your partner's voice with your own to establish a baseline of positive emotion.

With superior nonverbal language areas in her right-brain hemisphere, a woman senses anger and deception in a man's voice better than he does in hers.

We respond with specific emotions to specific vocal sounds. The three animal notes in your voice—growls, barks, and whines—

emerge as you become tense, angry, or upset. These ancient vocalizations send a disturbing message—"something is wrong"—and should be avoided in courtship. In its recent evolution for speech, the human voice became musically tonal. Psychologically, a voice's melodious intonations are pleasing to the ear. Since the right person deserves the right key, your partner should always hear a ring of excitement in your voice.

In courtship, hand-behind-head is a clear signal that "something is wrong."

The three animal notes in your voice—growls, barks, and whines—emerge as you become tense, angry, or upset. These ancient vocalizations send a disturbing message—"something is wrong"—and should be avoided in courtship.

A key to nonverbal communication is *redundancy*. Duplicating or repeating a message makes it more likely to be understood. Men commonly assume that after speaking in a loving key for the first few notes of a marital chat, they need not continue. Instead, they revert to lower tones used with fellow men. Women assume that when a man's tone of voice changes, his level of caring changes as well. He should use caring tones repeatedly to reassure her that he cares.

An effective way to show you care is to put down your newspaper, mute the TV, lean forward, and give eye contact as you listen to your partner's words. At the same time, watch for mood signs evident in lips, shoulders, and hands.

A SHARED LAUGH. The more you laugh together, the closer you become. Laughter is a whole-brain activity that involves areas of the primitive brain stem, centers of the motor and cognitive cerebral cortex, and pleasure areas of the frontal lobes, hypothalamus, and midbrain. In strong laughter, you see an open-mouth smile, involuntary spasms of the respiratory muscles, flaring nostrils, tearing eyes, facial flushing, and forward-bowing motions of the head and torso.

More than humorous, social laughter evolved in primates to strengthen companionate bonds. Today it works for us as it does for gorillas and chimps (Van Hooff, 1967). Emotionally, laughing together brings a shared feeling of exhilaration (Ruch, 1993). Physically, laughter lowers muscle tone and increases bodily relaxation. Chemically, laughter relieves stress as it releases euphoria-producing endorphins, enkephalins, dopamine, noradrenaline, and adrenaline. Socially, laughter binds you together as allies united against outsiders and forces beyond your control.

Laughter is contagious. On TV "canned laughter" stimulates in viewers an unconscious contagion of isopraxic chuckling. In courtship, the same-behavior principle unites laughing couples as they imitate each other's rhythmic vocalizations, facial expressions, and movements. As with touching, hugging, and a loving voice, daily doses of synchronous laughter significantly strengthen companionate love.

From PONS (Profile of Nonverbal Sensitivity) tests given to seven thousand subjects from nineteen countries. Harvard psychologist Robert Rosenthal found that people who read feelings from nonverbal cues are better adjusted, more outgoing, and more popular than those who cannot.

Communicate, Communicate, Communicate

Paraphrasing baseball's legendary Lawrence Peter ("Yogi") Berra, "Courtship ain't over till it's over." You exchange nonverbal signs, signals, and cues for the entirety of your relationship. Using this field guide to read your own and your partner's love signals can help you build the self-awareness required for a lively, enduring, empathetic relationship. May the knowledge and insights you gain from people watching bring you a soul mate for life.

BIBLIOGRAPHY

Alford, Richard (1996). "Adornment." In David Levinson and Melvin Ember, eds. *Encyclopedia of Cultural Anthropology* (New York: Henry Holt), pp. 7–9.

Amato, Ivan (1992). "In Search of the Human Touch," *Science* 258:27 (November): 1436–37.

Barber, Elizabeth (1994). *Women's Work: The First 20,000 Years* (New York: Norton).

Bastock, Margaret (1967). *Courtship: An Ethological Study* (Chicago: Aldine Publishing Co.).

Beck, S., Ward-Hull, C., and P. McLear (1976). "Variables Related to Women's Somatic Preferences of the Male and Female Body," *Journal of Personality and Social Psychology* 34: 1200–10.

Berman, Jennifer, and Laura Berman (2001). *For Women Only* (New York: Henry Holt).

Birren, F. (1978). *Color & Human Response* (New York: Van Nostrand Reinhold).

Blass, Elliott M. (1992). "The Ontogeny of Motivation: Opioid Bases of Energy Conservation and Lasting Affective Change in Rat and Human Infants," *Current Directions in Psychological Science* (August): 116–20.

Bradbury, Jack W., and Sandra L. Vehrencamp (1998). *Principles of Animal Communication* (Sunderland, Mass.: Sinauer Associates, Inc.).

Burgoon, Judee K. (1994). "Nonverbal Signals." In Knapp, Mark L., and Gerald R. Miller, eds. *Handbook of Interpersonal Communication*, 2nd ed. (London: Sage Publications), pp. 229–85.

Buss, David M. (1998). "Psychological Sex Differences: Origins Through Sexual Selection." In Clinchy, Blythe McV., and Julie K. Norem, eds. *The Gender and Psychology Reader* (New York: New York University Press), pp. 228–35.

Canary, Daniel J., and Tara M. Emmers-Sommer (1997). *Sex and Gender Differences in Personal Relationships* (New York: The Guilford Press).

Cappella, Joseph N. (1983). "Conversational Involvement: Approaching and Avoiding Others." In Wiemann, John M., and Randall P. Harrison, eds. *Nonverbal Interaction* (Beverly Hills: Sage Publications), pp. 113–48.

Carlson, Neil R. (1986). *Physiology of Behavior*, 3rd ed. (Boston: Allyn & Bacon).

Chartrand, T. L., and J. A. Bargh (1999). "The Chameleon Effect: The Perception-Behavior Link and Social Interaction," *Journal of Personality and Social Psychology* 76(6):893–910.

Cho, Emily, and Neila Fisher (1996). *Instant Style* (New York: Harper-Collins).

Crown, Lawrence (1987). *Marilyn at Twentieth Century Fox* (London: Comet Books).

Damasio, Antonio R. (1994). *Descartes' Error: Emotion, Reason, and the Human Brain* (New York: G. P. Putnam's Sons).

Darwin, Charles (1871). *The Descent of Man and Selection in Relation to Sex*. In Charles Darwin (N.D.) *The Origin of Species and The Descent of Man* (New York: Random House), pp. 387–924.

Darwin, Charles (1872). *The Expression of the Emotions in Man and Animals*, 3rd ed. (New York: Oxford University Press, 1998).

Dutton, D. G., and Arthur Aron (1974). "Some Evidence for Heightened Sexual Attraction Under Conditions of High Anxiety," *Journal of Personality and Social Psychology* 30: 510–17.

Eibl-Eibesfeldt, Irenaus (1970). *Ethology: The Biology of Behavior* (San Francisco: Holt, Rinehart, and Winston).

Fast, Julius (1970). *Body Language* (New York: M. Evans & Co., Inc.).

Field, A. E., L. Cheung, A. M. Wolf, D. B. Herzog, S. L. Gortmaker, and G. A. Colditz (1999). "Exposure to the Mass Media and Weight Concerns Among Girls," *Pediatrics* 103(3): e36.

Fincham, Frank D., Leyan O. L. Fernandes, and Keith Humphreys (1993). *Communicating in Relationships* (Champaign, Ill.: Research Press).

Goleman, Daniel (1995). *Emotional Intelligence* (New York: Bantam Books).

Grammer, Karl, W Schiefenhoevel, M. Schleidt, B. Lorenz, and I. Eibl-Eibesfeldt (1988). "Patterns on the Face: The Eyebrow Flash in Cross-cultural Comparison," *Ethology* 77: 279–99.

Gross, A. E. and C. Crofton (1977). "What Is Good Is Beautiful," *Sociometry* 40: 85–90.

Hall, Edward (1959). *The Silent Language* (Garden City, N.Y.: Anchor Books/Doubleday).

Hess, E. H. (1975). "The Role of Pupil Size in Communication," *Scientific American* 233: 110–19.

Hoebel, E. A. (1978). *The Cheyennes* (Chicago: Holt, Rinehart & Winston).

Hogbin, Ian (1964). *A Guadalcanal Society: The Kaoka Speakers* (New York: Holt, Rinehart & Winston).

Hopson, Janet (1980). "Growl, Bark, Whine & Hiss: Deciphering the Common Elements of Animal Language," *Science* 80 (May/June): 81–4.

Horne, Timothy, ed. (1995). *Gray's Anatomy: The Anatomical Basis of Medicine and Surgery,* 38th ed. (London: Churchill Livingstone).

Horvath, T. (1979). "Correlates of Physical Beauty in Men and Women," *Social Behavior and Personality* 7: 145–51.

Ingoldsby, Bron B. (1995). "Mate Selection and Marriage." In Bron B. Ingoldsby, and Suzanna Smith, eds. *Families in Multicultural Perspective* (New York: The Guilford Press), pp. 143–60.

Kandel, Eric R. (1991). "Perception of Motion, Depth, and Form." In Kandel, Eric R., James H. Schwartz, and Thomas M. Jessell, eds. *Principles of Neural Science,* 3rd ed. (Norwalk, Conn.: Appleton & Lange), pp. 440–66.

Kantowitz, Barry H., and Robert D. Sorkin (1983). *Human Factors* (New York: John Wiley & Sons).

Karson, Craig N. (1992). "Oculomotor Disorders in Schizophrenia." In Anthony B. Joseph, and Robert R. Young, eds. *Movement Disorders in Neurology and Neuropsychiatry* (Cambridge, Mass.: Blackwell Scientific Pubs.), pp. 414–421.

Kastor, Elizabeth (1994). "Head Over Heels," *Washington Post Magazine* (March 6): 28–30, 38.

Kevles, Bettyann (1986). *Females of the Species: Sex and Survival in the Animal Kingdom* (Cambridge: Harvard University Press).

Knapp, Mark L. (1972). *Nonverbal Communication in Human Interaction* (New York: Holt, Rinehart & Winston).

Korthase, K. M., and I. Trenholme (1982). "Perceived Age and Perceived Physical Attractiveness," *Perceptual and Motor Skills* 54: 1251–58.

LaFrance, Marianne, and Marvin A. Hecht (2000). "Gender and Smiling: A Meta-Analysis." In Agneta H. Fischer, *Gender and Emotion: Social Psychological Perspectives* (Cambridge: Cambridge University Press), pp. 118–42.

Langlois, Judith H., and Lori A. Roggman (1990). "Attractive Faces Are Only Average," *Psychological Science* 1 (2): 115–21.

LeVay, Simon (1993). *The Sexual Brain* (London: MIT Press).

Liebowitz, Michael R. (1983). *The Chemistry of Love* (Boston: Little, Brown).

Malinowski, Bronislaw (1929). *The Sexual Life of Savages in Northern Melanesia: An Ethnographic Account of Courtship, Marriage and Family Life Among the Natives of the Trobriand Islands, British New Guinea* (New York: Horace Liveright).

Manstead, Antony S. R. (1998). "Gender Differences in Emotion." In Blythe McV. Clinchy, and Julie K. Norem, eds. *The Gender and Psychology Reader* (New York: New York University Press), pp. 236–64.

Massey, Lorraine (2002). *Curly Girl* (New York: Workman).

Masters, William H., Johnson, Virginia E., and Robert C. Kolodny (1986). *Masters and Johnson on Sex and Human Loving* (Boston: Little, Brown).

May, J. L., and P. A. Hamilton (1980). "Effects of Musically Evoked Affect on Women's Interpersonal Attraction Toward and Perceptual Judgements of Physical Attractiveness of Men," *Motivation and Emotion* 4: 217–28.

Mehrabian, Albert (1967). "Orientation Behaviors and Nonverbal Attitude Communication," *Journal of Communication* 17: 324–32.

Mehrabian, Albert (1981). *Silent Messages: Implicit Communication of Emotions and Attitudes* (Belmont, Calif.: Wadsworth).

Mita, T. H., M. Dermer, and J. Knight (1977). "Reversed Facial Images and the Mere-Exposure Hypothesis," *Journal of Personality & Social Psychology* 13: 89–111.

Morris, Desmond (1967). *The Naked Ape* (New York: McGraw-Hill).

Morris, Desmond (1983). "Social Intimacy." In Albert M. Katz and Virginia T. Katz, eds. *Foundations of Nonverbal Communication* (Carbondale: Southern Illinois University Press), pp. 134–47.

Morris, Desmond (1994). *Bodytalk: The Meaning of Human Gestures* (New York: Crown).

Mowat, Farley (1987). *Woman in the Mists: The Story of Dian Fossey and the Mountain Gorillas of Africa* (New York: Warner Books).

Naumann, Earl (2001). *Love at First Sight: The Stories and Science Behind Instant Attraction* (Naperville, Ill.: Sourcebooks).

Nauta, Walle J. H., and Michael Feirtag (1979). "The Organization of the Brain." In Rodolfo R. Llinás, ed. *The Workings of the Brain: Development, Memory, and Perception (Readings from Scientific American Magazine, 1976–1987)* (New York: W. H. Freeman, 1990), pp. 17–36.

Ogilvie, M. A. (1978). *Wild Geese* (Vermillion, S. Dak.: Buteo Books).

Parton, Dolly (1994). *Dolly* (New York: HarperCollins).

Patzer, Gordon L. (1985). *The Physical Attractiveness Phenomena* (New York: Plenum Press).

Perrett, D. I., K. A. May, and S. Yoshikawa (1994). "Facial Shape and Judgements of Female Attractiveness," *Nature* 368:17 (March): 239–42.

Pond, Caroline M. (1997). "Biological Origins of Adipose Tissue in Humans." In Mary Ellen Morbeck, Alison Galloway, and Adrienne L.

Zihlman, eds. *The Evolving Female: A Life-History Perspective* (Princeton, N.J.: Princeton University Press), pp. 147–62.

Pope, Harrison G., Katharine A. Phillips, and Roberto Olivardia (2000). *The Adonis Complex: The Secret Crisis of Male Body Obsession* (New York: Free Press).

Porges, Stephen W. (1995). "Orienting in a Defensive World: Mammalian Modifications of Our Evolutionary Heritage. A Polyvagal Theory," *Psychophysiology* 32: 301–18.

Restak, Richard (1995): *Brainscapes* (New York: Hyperion).

Richmond, Virginia P., James C. McCroskey, and Steven K. Payne (1991). *Nonverbal Behavior in Interpersonal Relations,* 2nd ed. (Englewood Cliffs, N.J.: Prentice Hall).

Rodgers, Joann E. (2001). *Sex: A Natural History* (New York: W. H. Freeman).

Ruch, Willibald (1993). "Exhilaration and Humor." In M. Lewis, and J. M. Haviland, eds. *The Handbook of Emotion* (New York: Guilford Publications), pp. 605–16.

Sapir, Edward (1927). "The Unconscious Patterning of Behavior in Society." In David Mandelbaum, ed. *Selected Writings of Edward Sapir* (Los Angeles: University of California Press, 1958), pp. 544–59.

Savic, I., H. Berglund, B. Gulyas, and P. Roland (2001). "Smelling of Odorous Sex Hormonelike Compounds Causes Sex-Differentiated Hypothalamic Activations in Humans," *Neuron* 31(4): 661–68.

Stern, K., and M. K. McClintock (1998). "Regulation of Ovulation by Human Pheromones," *Nature* 392:177–79.

Stewart, Elizabeth G. (2002). *The V Book: A Doctor's Guide to Complete Vulvovaginal Health* (New York: Bantam Books).

Stewart, R. A., S. J. Tutton, and R. E. Steele (1973). "Stereotyping and Personality: I. Sex Differences in Perception of Female Physiques." In *Perceptual and Motor Skills* 36: 811–14.

Stoddart, D. Michael (1990). *The Scented Ape: The Biology and Culture of Human Odour* (Sydney: Cambridge University Press).

Symons, Donald (1979). *The Evolution of Human Sexuality* (New York: Oxford University Press).

Tennov, Dorothy (1979). *Love and Limerence: The Experience of Being in Love* (New York: Stein & Day).

Tyrangiel, Josh (2002). "Dating After Doomsday," *Time* (October 1), p. 107.

Van Hooff, J. (1967). "The Facial Displays of the Catarrhine Monkeys and Apes." In Desmond Morris, ed. *Primate Ethology* (Chicago: Aldine), pp. 7–68.

Vargas, Marjorie Fink (1986). *Louder than Words: An Introduction to Nonverbal Communication* (Ames: Iowa State University Press).

Vienne, Véronique (1997). "Reinventing the Rules," *Style* (September) 149–52, 154, 156, 158, 160.

Waal, Frans De (1982). *Chimpanzee Politics* (London: Jonathan Cape).

Waller, Willard (1937). "The Rating and Dating Complex," *American Sociological Review* (2): 727–37.

Walters, Mark Jerome (1988). *Courtship in the Animal Kingdom* (New York: Doubleday).

Zajonc, R. B. (1968). "Attitudinal Effects of Mere Exposure," *Journal of Personality and Social Psychology* (9): 1–27.